TEN DAYS IN THE DIRT

THE SPECTACLE OF OFF-ROAD MOTORCYCLING

RUSS ROHRER

MOTORBOOKS
INTERNATIONAL

WARNING

Off-road motorcycling is an extremely dangerous and sometimes fatal sport. All riders pictured in this book are professionals using proper protective gear under controlled conditions. Attempting to duplicate any of the maneuvers may be hazardous or fatal and is not recommended. Readers are cautioned that individual abilities, motorcycles, terrain, jumps, and riding conditions differ. Due to the unlimited factors beyond the control of the authors, riders quoted, and publishers, liability is expressly disclaimed. Do not attempt any maneuvers, stunts, or techniques beyond your capabilities.

Library of Congress Cataloging-in-Publication Data

Rohrer, Russ, 1963–
   Ten Days in the Dirt / by Russ Rohrer.
      p. cm.
   ISBN 0-7603-1803-4 (alk. paper)
   1. Motocross—United States. 2. Motorcycle racing—United States. I. Title.

GV1060.12.R64 2004
796.7'56—dc22

2004045417

On the front cover: (main)
Jimmy Lewis throwing roost on a KTM. *Joe Bonello*

(inset, left to right)
1. Ricky Carmichael on the Honda at the Anaheim Supercross 2003.

2. Look closely at the front tire being squashed under pressure. Although these tires don't have big knobbies like those used in motocross, the soft-compound tire still provides incredible traction at these slow speeds.

3. The ISDE is won or lost in the tests so it's crucial to go as fast as possible. U.S. Junior World Trophy team rider Wally Palmer uncorks. *Mark Kariya*

4. Chad Reed at Glen Helen in 2003.

Endpaper:
The future heroes of off-road doing battle at the Mini Grand Prix.

On the frontis:
The Big Buck GNCC. *Bryan Nylander*

On the title page:
World Mini GP.

On the back cover:
Dick Burleson on a trail ride in northern Ontario. *Lee Klancher*

On the front flap:
Ricky Carmichael and Ezra Lusk chat prior to the Anaheim Supercross.

Edited by Lee Klancher and Lindsay Hitch
Designed by Mandy Iverson

Printed in China

CONTENTS

FOREWORD

Every kid grows up dreaming of being the best at something. Some kids want to be the next Michael Jordan. Some want to be like baseball player Sammy Sosa, but for me, it was being the next Rick Johnson. I shared those dreams with a kid named Jeremy McGrath back in the late 1980s. After school I would drive to his parent's muffler shop in Murrietta, California, so we could ride in the field across the street. I was No. 124, he was No. 125, and fun was always the name of the game. We rode for the love of the sport, nothing more and nothing less.

Our careers soon took us in different directions. Jeremy went onto try his hand at racing, and I went on to become a journalist. I never would have imagined that I would spend the next decade documenting the unbelievable career of one of my best friends. McGrath went on to win 72 250cc AMA Supercross main events and seven titles—two records that may never be broken. He was also successful outdoors, winning a bunch of races and several titles, plus the prestigious Motocross des Nations. Jeremy served as a catalyst during the beginning of the freestyle movement and was an inspiration to all those who watched him ride. During his racing career, he was an innovator who helped open doors in corporate America and made the world take note of his favorite sport.

Jeremy was so successful that he expanded the opportunities for everyone around him. When I was a youngster, my father always told me to find something that I liked and make a career out of it. I liked riding motorcycles and was hell-bent on doing it for a living. My travels as a journalist have taken me all

over the world. I've been fortunate enough to ride in exotic places like Zimbabwe, Costa Rica, and Peru. I've ridden from Guadalajara to Puerto Vallarta, Mexico, in the islands of Hawaii, and in most of the continental United States. I've been fortunate enough to try my hand at several different aspects of the sport, including hill climbing, trials, cross-country racing, and the International Six Days Enduro. I've been lucky enough to learn that there isn't just one way to have fun on motorcycles. There are many extremes in the world of off-road, and all of them are capable of providing tons of fun.

I'm really proud that when kids go out riding like we did 15 years ago, they grow up hoping to be like my friend Jeremy McGrath. But what I think is the coolest thing of all, is that once he retired, MC was more excited about riding than ever. He wanted to experience things that he couldn't normally do because of the constraints of racing. It just proves that fun is unlimited, and you don't have to be a racer to enjoy the experience. This sport continues to bring me a lot of fun every day, and I hope you can enjoy it as well!

–Ken Faught

Editor-in-Chief, *Dirt Rider* Magazine

Ken Faught and Jeremy McGrath. Massimo Melani

INTRODUCTION

BLUE COLLAR HEROES

Not long ago, off-road racer Chuck Woodford was just out of college and working as a Sears appliance repair man. He scraped up a few bucks, bought a three-year-old race bike, and took it down to compete at a local off-road race. He ended up in the B (intermediate) class and won the class by 15 minutes.

Woodford kept decimating the competition in the lower classes, and pro racer Fred Andrews saw him race not long after that. Andrews realized the kid had potential and helped him get a newer bike to race. Within a year or so, Woodford was running with the elite in the Grand National Cross Country (GNCC) class. By 2003, Woodford had a factory contract with the Kawasaki off-road team and made his living racing bikes. It isn't a lavish amount—he's not going to make the millions of dollars available to top motocross racers—but he's making a living doing what he loves.

I had the pleasure of speaking to Woodford at an event early in 2004. He was happy to talk about his career, and was clearly thrilled to be living his dream. He's tremendously talented and dedicated, but you'd never know that talking with him. He comes across as just another motorcycle person.

Attending one of the events Woodford competes in, a GNCC race, you'll find that the fans and the participants are also motorcycle people. The guy cheering on the sidelines and the woman in the KTM t-shirt probably spend weekends racing as well, or perhaps just trail riding.

You'll find the crowd just as tightly related to the competitors at most of the events in this book. These events are packed with people cheering for others who do what they do, just faster.

The competitors themselves are not always full-time professionals. Motocross and supercross are the exceptions to this rule, but even in those competitions only the top few racers are making serious money. The bulk of the field is packed with competitors who take home about the same wage as the construction worker in the stands.

At an off-road race, most of the racers have day jobs and even the top guys still make less than most small company executives. These top-notch athletes are as dedicated and serious about their sport as our stick-and-ball heroes, but they remain as lunch-pail as can be. Stop and talk to Scott Summers or Mike Lafferty, two of the true heroes of off-road racing, and either one will take the time to shoot the breeze. Neither is encumbered by an oversized ego, and both can do things on a motorcycle that are as unbelievable as a Derek Jeter diving catch or a Brett Favre last-gasp shovel pass.

When our heroes have time for us yet do things we cannot, I figure that's the way life's supposed to be. And off-road racing is still pretty much that way. Yeah, now you can find top supercross and motocross stars doing the occasional mainstream ad and making appearances on *The Tonight Show* or *Late Show with David Letterman*, but the bulk of the population would still walk right by them on the street. You have to be in the know to consider these heroes as superstars, which means the sport hasn't become a machine that creates multi-millionaires who marry pop stars and have their personal lives splattered on the tabloids.

Ten Days in the Dirt takes you on a tour of the happily down-to-earth world of off-road racing. You'll spend ten days roosting with the best in the sport, from the highly-paid pros who leap 100-foot triple jumps in supercross racing to the seven-year-old racers who spend their nights and weekends practicing to become the next stadium superhero.

You'll travel to Brazil for an International Six Days Enduro, where competitors need the endurance of a marathon racer, the mechanical abilities of a race car technician, and the ability to save enough energy during a long race to put out sprinter-level energy during the special tests. A stop at a trials event gives you a look at the phenomenal bike control and balance exhibited by trials competitors, and a layover in Billings should prove to you that hillclimb racers are certifiably insane. You'll also visit a Grand National Cross Country, the grueling three-hour off-road race that requires stamina and mental toughness.

And at all these events, the fans—people with rider's names painted on their chests, funny hairdos, signs, and air horns to blow when their hero comes by—are most likely motorcycle people.

In fact, if you have this book in your hands, you are probably a motorcycle person, or perhaps you are considering becoming one. Either way, you've picked a great sport. And, as far as I'm concerned, you couldn't find better people.

I hope you enjoy the book. More importantly, I hope to see you on the trail.

—Lee Klancher
March 10, 2004

A rainy race day Sunday in South Carolina. Bryan Nylander

AMA SUPERCROSS SERIES

SECOND ONLY TO NASCAR?

Supercross is the most visible form of off-road motorcycle racing in the world and attracts a lot of international riders like KTM's Grant Langston. He won a 125cc World Championship before leaving his home in South Africa. Although he's only had limited success in supercross, he did win the 2003 AMA 125cc National Championship.

Name of Event:
AMA Supercross Series

Location:
Anaheim, California

Date:
January 4, 2003

Fan Attendance:
Sellout

Watching an off-road motorcycle race was extremely difficult during the first motorcycle boom in the 1970s. Desert racing was one of the more popular forms of competition, and fans could only see their favorite riders for a few minutes a day, at best. That was until promoter Mike Goodwin scribbled notes on a cocktail napkin with the unique idea of bringing a "Chunk of Baja" to Los Angeles. The city had constructed a 100,000-seat mega stadium, named the Los Angeles Coliseum in honor of the original built in Rome, and the sport of supercross was born.

Since the original race in 1972, the sport of stadium motocross has turned into the world's most visible form of motorcycle racing. In the 1970s and 1980s, the most prestigious titles were World Championships won on the Grand Prix circuit, run mostly in Europe. In the late 1980s and early 1990s, however, the sport underwent a major transformation when supercross athletes became a highly marketable commodity worldwide. Increased television coverage, outside sponsorship, and sellout crowds turned the 16-round series into a global phenomenon. It also turned racers into millionaires, which attracted athletes from around the world.

Course Length: Approximately 1/2 mile

Terrain: Big jumps spaced closely together combined with technical jumps and a treacherous whoop section.

Conditions: Perfect—about 70 degrees Fahrenheit in the afternoon and 60 at night. The Dirt Wurx crew, who built the track, did an excellent job of keeping the track tacky all evening during the most important races of the event.

Challenge: Avoiding costly mistakes. The obstacles are spaced so close together that a mistake can be very costly. Supercross is usually the least forgiving type of racing, since riders have two 70-foot triple jumps, plus a variety of combination jump sections to master.

125cc: 1. Travis Preston (Hon); 2. James Stewart (Kaw); 3. Andrew Short (Suz); 4. Chris Gosselaar (Hon); 5. Danny Smith (Suz); 6. Billy Laninovich (KTM); 7. Matt Walker (Kaw); 8. David Pingree (Suz); 9. Craig Anderson (Yam); 10. Kevin Johnson (Yam); 11. Shane Bess (Suz); 12. Joshua Hansen (Yam); 13. Tiger Lacey (Yam); 14. Turbo Reif (Hon); 15. Akira Narita (Suz); 16. Levi Reid (Suz); 17. K.raudo Toda (Hon); 18. Bryan McGavran (Suz); 19. Tyler Evans (Suz); 20. Ryan Morais (Suz).

250cc: 1. Chad Reed (Yam); 2. Ricky Carmichael (Hon); 3. Tim Ferry (Yam); 4. David Vuillemin (Yam); 5. Sebastien Tortelli (Suz); 6. Ernesto Fonseca (Hon); 7. Ryan Clark (Yam); 8. Ezra Lusk (Kaw); 9. Heath Voss (Yam); 10. Stephane Roncada (Suz); 11. Keith Johnson (Yam); 12. Ivan Tedesco (Yam); 13. Steve Boniface (KTM); 14. Larry Ward (Hon); 15. Darryl Hurley (Suz); 16. Mike Brown (Kaw); 17. Mike LaRocco (Hon); 18. Grant Langston (KTM); 19. Travis Pastrana (Suz); 20. Michael Byrne (Hon).

Results **Results**

The biggest event of the season is always the kickoff. Historically, round one has taken place in Anaheim, California, at Edison International Field, which is less than 2 miles from Disneyland. The season opener gives fans a chance to see which riders changed teams, who is debuting new technology, and, of course, who looks fast and who doesn't. Anaheim is a place where trends are born, rumors are dispelled, and Cinderella stories unfold. Riders have three months to heal from injuries sustained in the AMA National Championship MX Series, so this event always features tough competition.

Each new season charges the air with electricity. Riders are eager to prove themselves, and they ride more aggressively than ever. The first four rounds set the tone of the series. After those rounds it's usually easy to predict who will run for the championship once the series ends in May.

The supercross series has national prominence with stops in major U.S. cities. Starting in January, the tour visits Phoenix, San Francisco, Dallas, Houston, Detroit, Salt Lake City, San Diego, Atlanta, Daytona, Indianapolis, and Las Vegas.

The sport is divided into two classes, the most prestigious being the traditional 250cc class. However, the AMA rules allow much larger 450cc four-strokes to compete against 250cc two-strokes, which ruled the sport until 1997. That year, Yamaha debuted the YZ400F, and team rider Doug Henry took it to victory lane during its inaugural race in Las Vegas.

---

1 The first turn is arguably more important in supercross than in any other form of two-wheel racing. The tight confines of the stadium track make it difficult to pass. Riders in the 125cc class only have 15 laps to make forward progress, and 250cc riders only have 20. With lap times hovering around the one-minute mark, the pace is extremely fast.

2 Four-strokes have become extremely popular in the 125cc class, and are now considered the weapon of choice. They tend to launch out of the starting gate faster and maintain power in long whoop sections.

3 Line choice is very important on supercross tracks. Outside lines generally provide more momentum for the jumps but leave riders vulnerable for riders on the inside line to make a block pass.

4 As a kid growing up in Costa Rica, Ernesto Fonseca came to the United States on a regular basis to find more competition. His efforts were later rewarded when he earned a Honda factory ride. In 2003, he managed to avoid injuries and made a handful of podium visits.

1

The other class is divided into two regions: East and West. Again, the 125cc designation is a poor description, since 250cc four-strokes are a major force, but this class was created to give younger riders a chance to master supercross before racing against the veterans.

Supercross courses are different from anything else in motorcycle racing and require different riding techniques. The tight confines of sports stadiums give track builders a limited amount of space. Obstacles are spaced closer together than on higher-speed motocross tracks. Jumps are steeper and catapult riders farther, as much as 70 feet in distance and 18 feet high. The short approach to these obstacles makes for some interesting riding techniques, and has allowed riders to link several obstacles together in jump combinations. To slow down the riders, track builders create whoops, which resemble moguls in skiing. These 3-foot-high mounds of dirt are spaced a few feet apart, and can be placed in sections as long as 65 yards. This provides an excellent opportunity on an otherwise tight track. The whoops and the larger combination jumps usually separate the winners from the losers, and the ability to triple jump areas that other riders can only double jump is a huge advantage in this extreme sport.

If riders get a bad start in the main event, they only have 20 laps in the 250cc class to improve their position, and 125cc riders only have 15. Lap times are usually one minute, and passing is really difficult because the course is less than 20 feet wide in most sections.

So the start usually provides the most action. The expression "no risk, no reward" couldn't be more applicable than in turn one. A rider who grabs the early lead has an unobstructed shot at each obstacle and is able to set the pace. Riders in the middle and the back of the pack usually can't do the big jumps because of the thick traffic that lies ahead.

Only a few riders have dominated the sport in the last three decades. Bob Hannah was the original supercross sensation in the late 1970s. Mark Barnett and the famous rivalry between Jeff Ward and Rick Johnson followed in the 1980s. Jeff Stanton won three championships before Jeremy McGrath arrived on the scene in 1993. McGrath went on to win 72 main events and seven championships. The year 2000 saw the end of McGrath's domination. Although he was beaten in 1997 by Kawasaki's Jeff Emig, it was a freckle-faced kid named Ricky Carmichael from Florida who would terminate the king's run. Carmichael won three consecutive titles (2001-2003), but this past year a new challenger arose. Australian Chad Reed won the season kickoff at Anaheim and went on to win eight of the 16 rounds. Ezra Lusk managed to win one main event, while Carmichael only won seven. Carmichael's consistency earned him the title, but many wonder if it will be his last. Reed proved that he's more aggressive, more confident, and the faster of the two, but there's a third factor that will affect the future of supercross— an 18-year-old superstar from Florida named James Stewart. This

---

1

World Champion Mickael Pichon competed at Anaheim as a warm-up race for the Grand Prix series in Europe. It was the first time he raced in the United States since Honda fired him under controversial circumstances several years earlier. After he got his walking papers, Pichon returned home to France and has repeatedly considered making a fulltime comeback to the American racing scene.

2

Yamaha hired Tim Ferry to promote its big-bore four-stroke, and the former 125cc Eastern Region Champ had his hands full with the massive dose of power.

3

Ten-time AMA Champion Ricky Carmichael won the Supercross title in 2003 even though many considered Chad Reed to be the fastest rider.

phenom—the most technical rider the sport has ever seen—was able to jump obstacles on a 125 that none of the riders on more powerful 250s were able to clear. "I think there's a chance that Reed may never win a title," said McGrath at the 2003 series finale in Las Vegas. "Reed is incredibly fast, and should have won the title instead of RC, but that may have been his last real shot. Both he and Ricky are going to have to up their game in order to beat Stewart."

"America is where all the action is," says Chad Reed. "I grew up watching Jeremy McGrath on television, and a supercross title is the only thing I've ever wanted. To me nothing else compares."

"The future of supercross is incredible," says Ken Faught, editor-in-chief of *Dirt Rider* magazine. "It's getting more mainstream attention than ever before. It's not uncommon to see photographers from *Sports Illustrated* on the field, and there are a lot of celebrity fans. I've seen Matt LeBlanc, William Shatner, Lyle Lovett, Ken Griffey Jr., Fabio, Angie Everhart, and Pamela Anderson at the races . . . there are really too many to list. In order for the sport to really grow in popularity, we really need another rider like McGrath. Hopefully, James Stewart is the kid to fill the void. He's got a great personality, understands how to win championships, and knows how to entertain crowds."

Throughout the first half of the 16-race series, Ricky Carmichael set the pace, but then Reed began to rise to the challenge. Reed won the last seven races of the season as Carmichael opted to take the safe route. Although Carmichael had the speed to battle Reed, the older Carmichael gave Reed plenty of room to avoid any on-track collisions that could jeopardize his championship run. In the end, Carmichael won the title, but Reed gained a lot of respect from the fans. Unfortunately for Carmichael, he underwent knee surgery at the end of the year and was unable to defend his title in 2004.

Teenage superstar James Stewart represents the future of our sport. He's changing the way we ride, and he constantly pushes the limits of what people consider possible on a motorcycle. Although he races in the 125cc class to gain experience, he's often referred to as the world's fastest all-around rider, and he's only 18.

The McGrath Supercross Dynasty

The 1993 AMA Supercross season began just like any other. There was a lot of preseason hype about the title favorites and the graduating kids from the 125cc class ready to knock them off. Under normal circumstances, this was nothing more than fodder created by race promoters who wanted to sell more tickets. But in 1993, there really was a changing of the guard, when a legitimate battle began between the seasoned veteran Jeff Stanton and a rookie 250cc rider named Jeremy McGrath.

Nicknamed "Showtime," McGrath won two 125cc Western Region SX Championships during the previous year and was already a talented stadium rider. As the checkered flag dropped on the 16-race series, it was the youngster from Murrietta, California, who earned the coveted blue-and-gold No. 1 plate. McGrath went on to win four consecutive supercross titles before Jeff Emig managed to dethrone him; but Emig only temporarily derailed McGrath's progress. Many believe that McGrath might have won the 1997 season had he not had a disagreement with Honda management. It was a falling-out that ended with McGrath switching to Team Suzuki just two weeks before the season started—a move that shocked the racing world. During the first race of the season, at the Los Angeles Memorial Coliseum, McGrath was taken out in the first turn by his former Honda teammate Steve Lamson. McGrath's problems escalated when he learned his new Wyatt Seals–tuned Suzuki couldn't be ridden the same way as his Honda. The RM250's clutch couldn't tolerate the abuse McGrath dished out. Although Suzuki found a fix in an eight-disc clutch, they were already deep into the season by the time the problem was solved. Then came a flat tire during the main event in Charlotte and a cut foot before the series finale in Las Vegas. Still, McGrath only lost the title by seven points.

A year earlier, in 1996, McGrath won all but one race during the series. His record-setting performance was nothing short of dominance defined. In 1998, he switched to Team Yamaha's satellite team, operated by the world's largest motorcycle shop, Chaparral, in San Bernardino, California. McGrath went on to win the title three more times in a row.

Seven AMA Supercross titles make Jeremy McGrath the greatest stadium racer of all time. In 1996, McGrath even won all but one race during the season and then took the No. 1 plate to team Suzuki.

Around the start of the new millennium, McGrath bought his own half-million-dollar semi in order to run a race team backed by Yamaha. But another 125cc rider named Ricky Carmichael was beginning to come into his own. Carmichael edged out McGrath in 2001 and 2002. Losing had never been a part of McGrath's racing career, and he knew he had to make some radical changes in his racing program.

McGrath was having contract negotiation problems with Yamaha when a deal from KTM fell into his lap. After coming to terms with the Austrian manufacturer, McGrath suffered a serious string of bad luck. He was knocked out during a non-series race in Italy, and he then dislocated his hip during a testing accident at KTM's private supercross track. A $10 check valve in the gas tank vent hose was inadvertently turned the wrong way and caused the motor to stall on the face of a 70-foot triple jump. McGrath, his family, and his team had no idea that this was the beginning of the end.

In January 2003, McGrath unexpectedly announced his retirement a day before the season was to begin. During a press conference at Anaheim Stadium with all the media and every current supercross star in attendance, McGrath told the world that he no longer felt like he was competitive. Fighting back tears, the seven-time champion announced that he had ridden his last stadium event.

"I've always raced because I enjoyed it," says McGrath. "I'm just a competitive person and never looked at it as a job. I always told myself that I would never race for second place, and I was true to my word. I know that I turned down a lot of money, but it was never about that. My motivation was always the fans and the thrill of the moment. I'm one of the biggest showoffs, and entertaining the crowd is what I'll miss most about racing."

"There's no way that anyone can measure how much McGrath did for our sport," says Ken Faught, editor-in-chief of Dirt Rider magazine. "He had a sense of style and charisma that may never be matched. He was the reason that fans filled 70,000-seat stadiums. They would stand in lines for hours just to get an autograph and a picture with the biggest champ. He dominated during the most competitive seasons in history, and now there is a distinct void."

7-time AMA 250cc Supercross Champion
(1993–1996, 1998–2000)

2-time AMA 125cc Western Region SX Champion
(1991–1992)

1-time AMA 250cc	National MX Champion (1995)
72 AMA 250cc	Supercross wins
13 AMA 125cc	Western Region SX wins
2 AMA 125cc	National Championship wins
15 AMA 250cc	National Championship wins

McGrath's Main Title Rivals

1993 Jeff Stanton and Mike Kiedrowski
1994 Mike LaRocco and Mike Kiedrowski
1995 Mike LaRocco
1996 Absolutely no one!
1997 Jeff Emig / Slipping Suzuki Clutch
1998 Jeff Emig and Ezra Lusk
1999 Ezra Lusk
2000 Ricky Carmichael and David Vuillemin
2001 Arm pump or severe tightening of the forearm muscles/every factory rider/top privateers (riders who have to spend their own money to compete)

Facts

- Jeremy never missed starting a 250cc Supercross between 1993 and 2002.
- Jeremy was 31 years old when he retired.
- The 2002 season was the first time in his career that McGrath didn't win at least one race.
- McGrath never won a 125cc East/West SX Shootout.
- Going into the 2003 season, McGrath was still the world's most popular rider even though he didn't race.
- McGrath owns Clutch Films (producers of the Steel Roots series) with best friend Lawrence Lewis.
- Jeremy has raced as a pro for all five major manufacturers.
- Skip Norfolk has been with McGrath since his professional career began (except for a short stint where Randy Lawrence and Wyatt Seals spun wrenches for McGrath).

Intimidation was one of McGrath's secret tactics. He was so good at it that many riders felt like they were racing for second once the gate dropped.

Confidence was always one of McGrath's strong points, especially in the whoops and on big jumps. The more precise his technique, the more precise his style, and the more often do jumps on the second or third lap in the race. Gray and McGrath that many riders would never do in the race. Fran Kuhn

Larry Ward started his professional racing career in the late 1980s and is still competitive. There are several riders who are racing well into their 30s, partially due to better safety equipment.

1 The 125cc class is divided into East and West regions and is designed to groom up-and-coming talent like Travis Preston for the 250cc class.

2 During the 2003 season, Ezra Lusk was the only rider aside from Ricky Carmichael and Chad Reed to pull off a win. It was his last win as a Team Chevy Trucks Kawasaki factory rider. Joe Bonnello

1

GRAND NATIONAL
CROSS COUNTRY SERIES

SPRINTING FOR THREE HOURS

Name of Event:
Big Buck GNCC

Location:
Union, South Carolina

Date:
April 12-13, 2003

Fan Attendance:
3,000

O ff-road racing comes in all shapes and sizes in the United States, but because of the factor support and the level of talent that competes, the most important event is the Grand National Cross Country Series run on the East Coast. It's here that America's top off-road heroes do battle on 8- to 12-mile-long courses for three hours nonstop. The racetracks themselves take riders through dense woods, up and down hills, through water crossings, and usually on a motocross track. The tracks are laid out a short time before the event, so riders don't have an opportunity to practice before their race.

Because of the total distance involved, usually 100 miles, the race requires physical stamina and mental composure. Unlike motocross that is dominated by teenage and early 20s adrenaline junkies, the off-road series competitors are typically a little older. In fact, most of the top riders are between 25 and 40 years old.

"Most kids want to ride motocross," says former AMA 125/250cc National MX Champion Mike

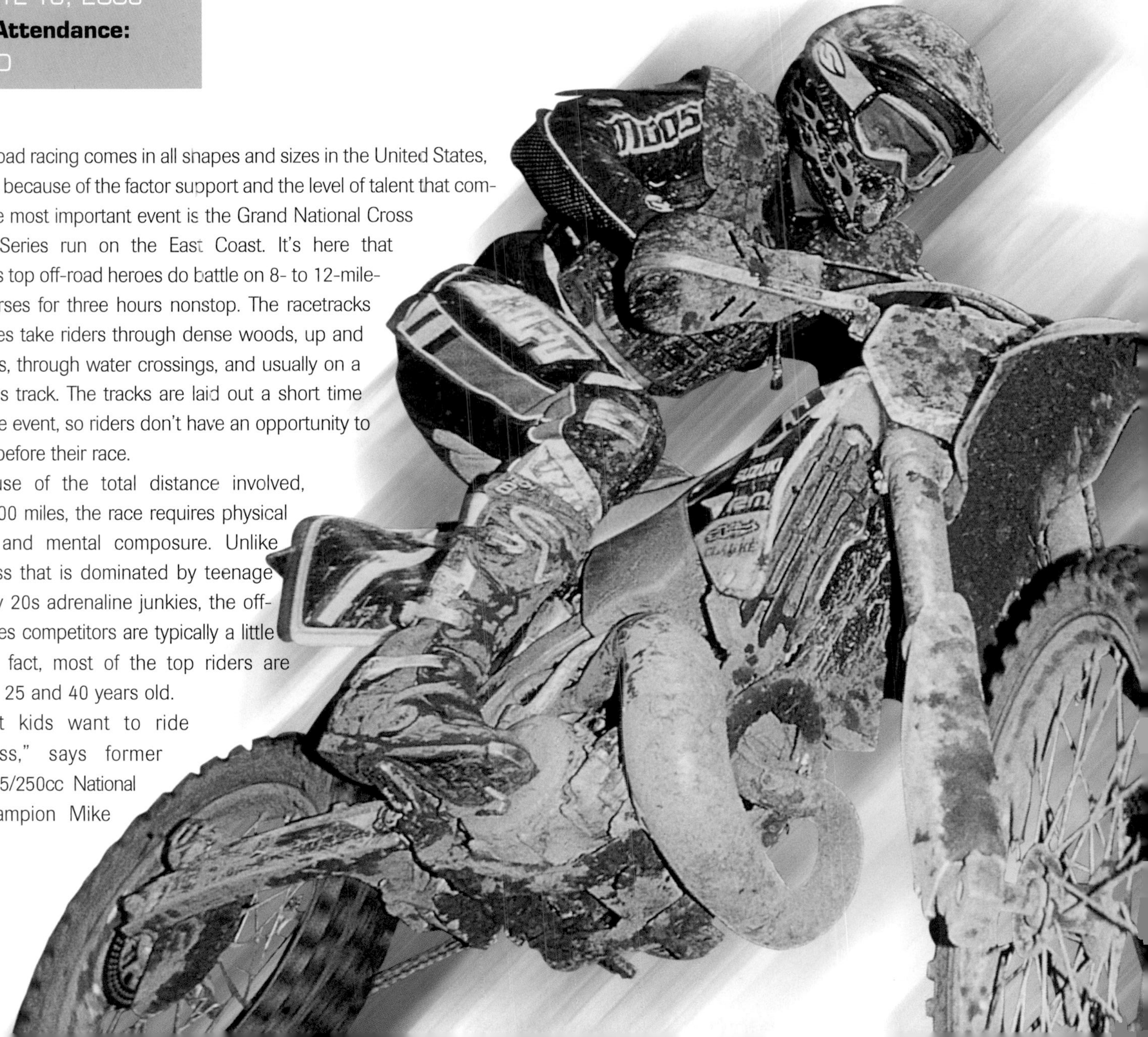

There are not a lot of jumps on the course, but when there is a good one, riders always like to flash a little style for spectators and photographers. Bryan Nylander

1

Riders start on rows, usually 20 riders a piece. For this type of racing, it's important to use handguards to protect your fingers and carry a drink system to reduce fatigue. Beneath the rider's neck, you can see a small clear tube that connects to a 2-quart drink system carried on the rider's back. Bryan Nylander

2

The terrain at a GNCC is very mixed. There are some wide-open areas, but there are also a lot of tight single tracks like this section being ridden by Patrick Garrahan, one of the top KTM riders. Bryan Nylander

Results

Course Length: Approximately 11 miles

Terrain: Tight woods, fields, creek crossings, rocks, and hill climbs on clay soil. Usually it has a spectacular creek jump where the pro riders launch off a bank and over the water (with a path around the jump for those who aren't as comfortable with air time).

Conditions: Can be rough and rutted and slippery if the clay is wet.

Challenge: The field sections are fast, fast, fast, and they get chopped up and rough as the week-end goes on, so you need to have your suspension sorted for that.

1. Fred Andrews; 2. Jason Raines; 3. Rodney Smith; 4. Michael Lafferty; 5. Barry Hawk; 6. Steve Hatch; 7. Joshua McLevy; 8. Randy Hawkins; 9. Jim Jarrett; 10. Robbie Jenks.

Kiedrowski. "Motocross and supercross get all the press and have all the big jumps that look spectacular. Off-road racing is more technical and really requires a lot of maturity. You can't be a quitter, and it's sometimes hard to find the motivation to ride for three hours."

However, most of the top off-road riders are past motocross racers. Ty Davis won the 125cc Western Region SX Series, Rodney Smith finished second in the 250cc World Championship in his prime, and Mike Kiedrowski was a motocross star in the late 1980s and early 1990s.

"Having a motocross background is good," says Smith. "When the series first started, it was modeled after the enduro series. Riders wore fanny packs, paced themselves better, and there wasn't much money involved. Now, the series has turned out to be a three-hour sprint race. You can't afford to work on your bike if you want to be in the top 10 of the professional class. You have to have good pit support, and everything has to be well choreographed. There's also a lot more money involved, which means people try harder, and there's real racing going on. It's not uncommon for one of these races to be won or lost by a few seconds. Think of that—100 miles of racing can come down to losing by 50 feet. Motocross teaches riders how to make aggressive passes and how to plan ahead."

In fact, top riders in the GNCC series can now make upwards of $300,000 a year, and teams like Suzuki and Yamaha have semis that transport team equipment to each round.

"There's always a lot of talk as to who really is the fastest off-road rider in the United States," says Ken Faught, editor-in-chief of *Dirt Rider* magazine. "It seems that more and more riders are leaving enduros and hare scrambles behind for the GNCC Series. Money has a way of attracting talent, and the talent pool is really deep in this form of racing."

"The racing is fun, and that's what attracts the riders," says Steve Hatch of Team Suzuki. "The promoters have turned it into a series that really tests riders and rewards those who are the most prepared. You can't just show up at a GNCC and 'luck' into a win, and since the terrain and conditions change so much, it really highlights the best overall rider."

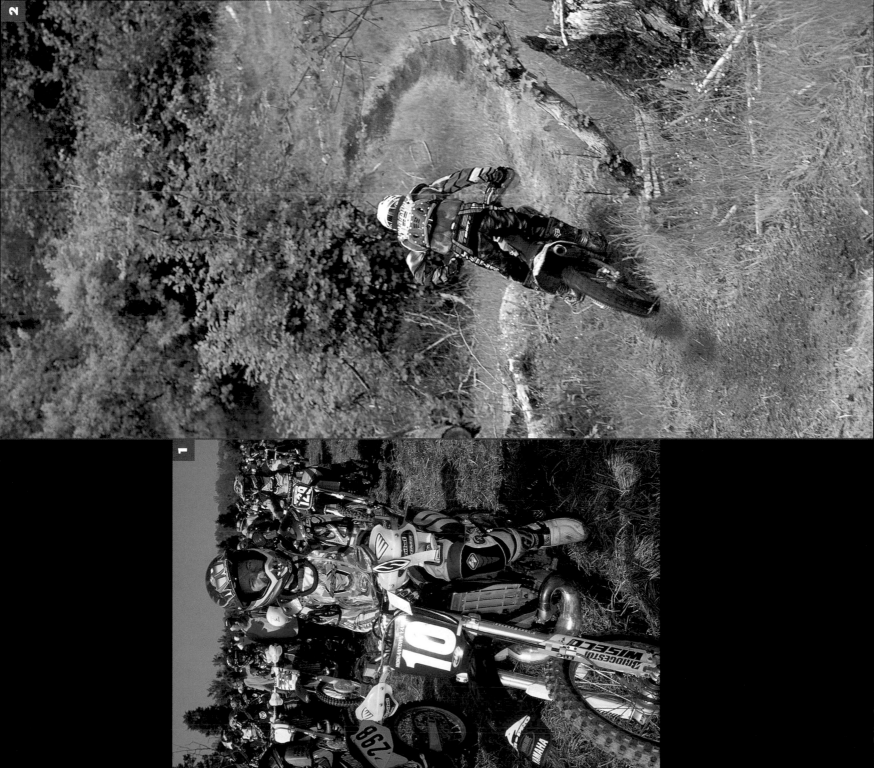

2 *Mud causes deep ruts that Fred Andrews is trying to avoid. Notice that his bike is steaming from all the water being splashed onto the pipe and engine. Andrews won Big Buck for Team Kawasaki, but in 2004 he's switching to Suzuki's program. Karel Kramer*

1 *Most GNCC courses are about 8 miles long and are lined with trees. Bryan Nylander*

The biggest problem with GNCC racing seems to be the question of cheating. Although cheaters are rarely caught or punished, there are a lot of accusations thrown around the pro ranks. The problem usually centers on course layout, where two parts of the track come together, yet are still separated by trees or brush so as not to make a shortcut so obvious. But with so much money on the line for race wins, championships, and sponsor bonuses, there can be a lot of finger pointing. It's easy to see why another rider would get upset—if he got a better start than an opponent, only to find out that he finished behind the rider without ever seeing him pass on the narrow course. Some years this seems to be more problematic than others, but the promoters are trying their best to get this under control.

To curb the problem, promoters have placed more spotters along the course and have instigated several checkpoints on each track. Using an electronic bar code scanner, race officials are able to see who went through what checkpoints at what time in order to spot anomalies. If a rider were to suddenly shave 15 percent of his point-to-point time, and were way faster than anyone else, it's a good indication that some foul play may have taken place. Although there are accusations every once in a while, the problem has become less of an issue now that riders don't know exactly when they're being monitored.

1

Check out these 14-inch ruts. When tracks get like this, conditions change every lap, and if you have problems, you had better get out of the way quickly or you'll get run over. Bryan Nylander

2

The ground can only absorb so much water so fast before the track turns into a small lake, but the racing continues. Bryan Nylander

The racing itself is intense and fun to watch. Each event begins with dead-engine start, and as many as 40 riders drag race to the first turn. The first few laps run at a sprint race as riders struggle for position. The middle half of the race runs with less intensity because the pecking order is generally determined by this time. It's during the last 45 minutes that riders bump up their pace in order to improve position.

"There's definitely a lot of strategy that goes into racing the GNCC series," says past champion Shane Watts. "You don't want to get stuck in the woods behind a lot of slower riders because that will enable the faster guys to break away. You want to keep your competition in sight, and then figure out when to make your move. There's a time when you want to conserve energy and a time when you need to ride on the edge. I think the GNCC Series offers the most intense off-road racing in the United States, and that's why I think it's attracting so many riders from other aspects of motorcycle racing."

1

1 Steady throttle and clutch control is the only way to get through tough sections like this. Notice that there is actually a line beneath this rider's left foot from all the riders paddling through the section, using their feet as outriggers. Bryan Nylander

2 There are all sorts of hazards like this stump on the outskirts of the track. One wrong move, and you're done for the day in GNCC racing. Bryan Nylander

3 Barry Hawk (No. 6) won the GNCC title for 2003. Bryan Nylancer

1

Each GNCC draws 400–600 riders each weekend. Bryan Nylander

2

Being uncomfortable is a part of off-road racing. To endure these types of elements, you have to be physically tough and mentally strong. Karel Kramer

3

Combine steep uphills with muddy ruts, and you've got a recipe for trouble. Bryan Nylander

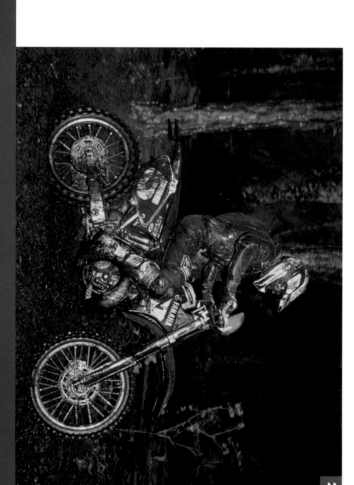

3

DAY 3

NMA WORLD MINI GRAND PRIX

KIDS AT PLAY

Name of Event:
NMA World Mini Grand Prix

Location:
Las Vegas, Nevada

Date:
April 17-20, 2003

Fan Attendance:
5,000

Everyone has their own reasons for diving into the world of racing. Some do it for the adrenaline rush, others do it for the camaraderie, while a few do it in search of fame and fortune. The amateur motocross circuit is the melting pot for two-wheel competition. On any given weekend, there are 250 races in the United States. Most of these races only have a hundred or so riders vying for a small trophy, but there are a few races that attract factory talent scouts in search of the next Jeremy McGrath, Ricky Carmichael, James Stewart, or Travis Pastrana. There are the Grand National Championships in both Mosier Valley, Texas, and Ponca City, Oklahoma; the Youth Amateur Nationals in Hurricane Mills, Tennessee; the Mini Olympics in Gainesville, Florida; and the World Mini Grand Prix in Las Vegas. There is not a top-20 American motocross rider today that hasn't raced some, if not most, of these events.

The annual World Mini Grand Prix attracts over 2,700 entrants riding everything from 50cc minibikes to big-bore 450cc four-strokes. They come as young as five years old and as old as 50, and they stay for four days in sweltering 100-degree heat from sunup to sundown. Forty riders simultaneously do battle on a man-made hybrid track comprised of supercross-style whoops and jumps, run at what is traditionally known as "outdoor speed." The spacing of the

Course Length: 5/8 mile

Terrain: Hard-pack dirt with lots of small stadium-style jumps. The facility is compact and offers excellent viewing.

Conditions: 100-degree temperatures and very dry air. The promoter watered the track often to keep dust down and increase traction.

Challenge: Getting a good start. The races are short, and a top-five start is usually needed to net a win.

50 STK (1-6): 1. Adam Cianciarulo (Cob); 2. Bradley Taft (Cob); 3. Brandon Olivares (Pol).
50 MOD (1-6): 1. Adam Cianciarulo (Cob); 2. Cade Moore (KTM); 3. Mike Victorian (Cob).
50 STK (7-8): 1. Zachary Bell (Cob); 2. Austin Aguilar (KTM); 3. Gavin Trettel (Cob).
50 MOD (7-8): 1. Gavin Trettel (Cob); 2. Caden Hadley (KTM); 3. Cody Thomas (Cob).
S/PW (6-9): 1. Grant Ransdell (KTM); 2. A.J. Catanzaro (Pol); 3. Zachary Bell (Cob).
65 STK (6-8): 1. Gavin Trettel (Suz); 2. Jesse Wentland (KTM); 3. Zachary Bell (Kaw).
65 MOD (6-8): 1. Jesse Wentland (KTM); 2. Jessy Nelson (KTM); 3. Mason Gragg (KTM).
65 STK (9-11): 1. Michael Hall (Kaw); 2. Landon Currier (KTM); 3. Nick Paluzzi (Kaw).
65 MOD (9-11): 1. Michael Leib (Kaw); 2. Landon Currier (KTM); 3. Chris Plouffe (Kaw).
65 OPEN (1-11): 1. Michael Hall (Kaw); 2. Jason Anderson (Kaw); 3. Levi Hall (KTM).
85 STK (1-11): 1. Ben LaMay (Suz); 2. Michael Hall (Kaw); 3. Chris Thies (Suz).
85 MOD (1-11): 1. Ben LaMay (Suz); 2. Tommy Weeck (Suz); 3. Dean Wilson (Kaw).
85 STK (12-13): 1. Zach Osbourne (KTM); 2. Josh Hill (Yam); 3. Kyle Cunningham (Kaw).
85 MOD (12-13): 1. Josh Hill (Yam); 2. Zach Osbourne (KTM); 3. Nico Izzi (Suz).
85 STK (14-16): 1. Mike Alessi (Hon); 2. Jeff Alessi (Hon); 3. Jordan Mockridge (Yam).
85 MOD (14-16): 1. Mike Alessi (Hon); 2. Ryan Villopoto (Kaw); 3. Jeff Alessi (Hon).
85 OPEN MOD: 1. Mike Alessi (Hon); 2. Ryan Villopoto (Kaw); 3. Nico Izzi (Suz).
S/MINI (1-16): 1. Mike Alessi (Hon); 2. Jeff Alessi (Hon); 3. Ryan Villopoto (Kaw).
125 OPEN NON-PRO: 1. Davi Millsaps (Suz); 2. Kyle Chisholm (Kaw); 3. Jarred Browne (Suz).
125 STK BEG: 1. Steven Hembree (Yam); 2. Brian Broughton (Yam); 3. Scott Martin (Suz).
125 MOD BEG: 1. Brian Broughton (Yam); 2. Philip Dowell (Yam); 3. Barry Humes (Yam).
125 STK NOV: 1. Brandon Kealamakia (Yam); 2. Jared Morrison (Yam); Jace Lewis (Hon).
125 MOD NOV: 1. Clay Higgins (Kaw); 2. Brock Harden (KTM); 3. Ricky James (Yam).
125 STK INT: 1. Joshua Lichtle (Suz); 2. Charlie Morrison (Yam); 3. Davi Millsaps (Suz).
125 MOD INT: 1. Joshua Lichtle (Suz); 2. Kyle Partridge (Suz); 3. Davi Millsaps (Suz).
125 STK PRO: 1. Jacob Saylor (Yam); 2. Cole Siebler (Yam); 3. Richie Owens (Kaw).
125 MOD PRO: 1. Evan Laughridge (Suz); 2. Brian Gray (Suz); 3. Bryan Johnson (Kaw).
250 STK NOV: 1. Kyle Summers (KTM); 2. Cory Redenius (Yam); 3. Kyle Calderini (Yam).
250 MOD NOV: 1. Andro Korlaet (Hon); 2. Cory Redenius (Yam); 3. Chad Geib (Suz).
250 STK INT: 1. Kyle Partridge (Suz); 2. Joshua Lichtle (Suz); 3. Eric McCrummen (Kaw).
250 MOD INT: 1. Joshua Lichtle (Suz); Kyle Chisholm (Kaw); 3. Kyle Partridge (Suz).
250 STK PRO: 1. Jacob Saylor (Yam); 2. Evan Laughridge (Suz); 3. Cole Siebler (Yam).
250 MOD PRO: 1. Jacob Saylor (Yam); 2. Evan Laughridge (Suz); 3. Brian Gray (Suz).
30+ OPEN B: 1. Kevin Cozadd (Suz); 2. Matt Tedder (Hon); 3. Damon Wasden (Hon).

---

obstacles is much wider than a normal super-cross and the jumps are smaller, which allows riders an easier time to successfully conquer each obstacle.

Honda, Suzuki, Yamaha, and KTM all have technicians on hand to offer emergency trackside assistance to riders. These are the same people who are looking for up-and-coming talent that might someday end up in a factory semi earning a seven-figure salary.

"This is a very important race for a lot of these young kids," says Eric Crippa of American Honda. "If you want to be a champion, you can't run away from the competition, you have to run towards it. The racers at the World Mini represent the best amateur riders, period. There can be a lot of pressure on these kids, and we look for the kids who seem like they have the best all-around package. There are no accidental champions in motocross racing. You have to eat, sleep, and breathe racing to be the best."

Mike and Jeff Alessi are two young riders from Southern California who have gained a lot of attention in the amateur circuit, and Honda has its eye on them as future superstars in the sport.

"It's not uncommon to see 12-year-olds training and worried about their diet," says Scot Harden of KTM, a former hero rider in the world of enduro racing. "This is a very demanding sport, and only the strongest survive. The races in Las Vegas only last 15 minutes, but you can't afford to have your lap times drop off at all. These are sprint races, and physical fitness is extremely important."

1 Most of the manufacturers post contingency for amateur riders.

2 Many of the factory teams send talent scouts to recruit up-and-coming riders like Davi Millsaps. His amateur career was so successful that when he made his pro debut at the Minneapolis Supercross in 2004, he was a full-fledged, salaried factory rider.

3 Pee Wee sales have skyrocketed since the mid-1990s. Some of the bikes are incredibly sophisticated even though they only have 50cc two-stroke engines designed for kids just starting school.

1

Once riders move up to the AMA Nationals, they will race two 40-minute motos a day, plus practice. They will spend about two hours on the bike during race days, and the conditions on the East Coast can be brutal. The heat and humidity zaps your energy and interferes with your concentration. If you are not physically and mentally fit, you are nothing in this sport.

"I've been covering the World Mini GP since the mid-1980s, and I've seen a lot of fast kids use the event as a launching pad for their careers," says Ken Faught, editor-in-chief of *Dirt Rider* magazine. "I remember watching Jeremy McGrath battle with Ryan Hughes on 125s, Ricky Carmichael dominate the 80 class, and James Stewart being undefeated on 60s. Each of these kids stood out from the rest of the riders. They were special, and they all knew it."

Families play a huge role in the success of young riders. In most cases the entire family dynamic revolves around racing. The sport is expensive and most kids can't do it without serious financial support. Riding and racing are privileges, and many parents use racing as a tool to improve grades and keep their kids out of trouble.

"I remember Jeremy McGrath's dad coming home from work, eating dinner, and going out in the garage to work on his bikes until he went to sleep. He did it five days a week and then traveled on the weekend to attend races," Faught says.

Because of the expense of racing, Yamaha introduced race contingency in 1985 in the form of "YZ Bucks." These are gift certificates redeemable at local Yamaha dealers for parts and accessories. Today, manufacturers offer approxi-

1 Racing at big amateur events like the World Mini Grand Prix is still very intense. A lot of kids realize that they can make a career out of racing if they have the talent and financial backing.

2 Kids travel from all over the world to race at big events like the World Mini Grand Prix. Unlike traditional stick-and-ball sports, motocross is very expensive at all levels, even casual recreational riding. Add entry fees, travel expenses, and performance parts, and racing can cost over $100,000 a year, even as an amateur.

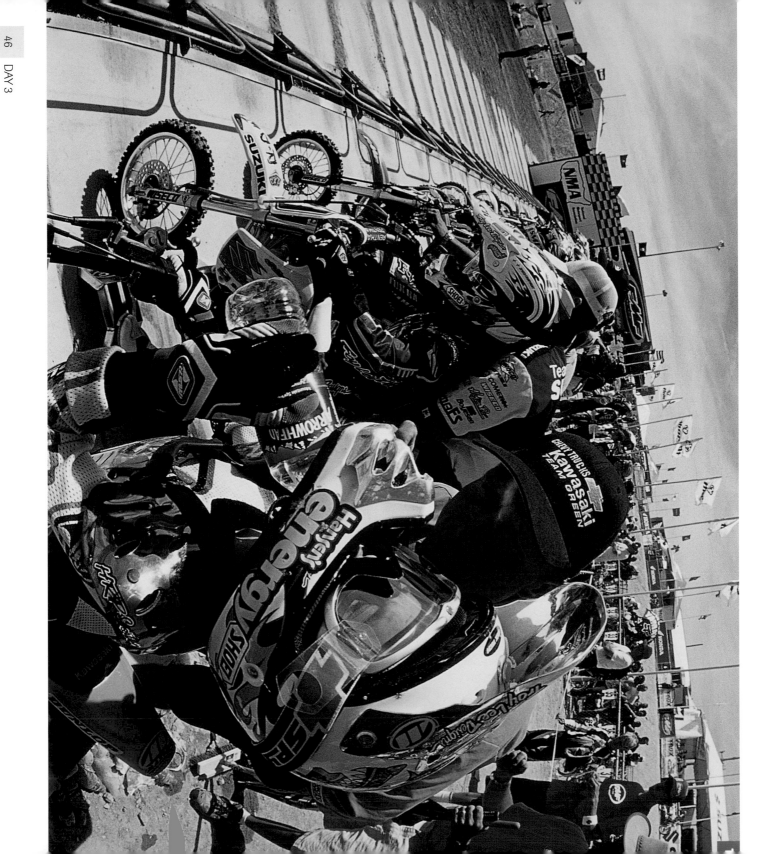

mately $20 million for motocross, supercross, off-road, and road racing in the United States alone. There's enough money out there that top amateur riders can even profit from their racing careers thanks to clothing contracts, contingency, and manufacturer support. This is the exception, not the norm, but money continues to change the sport. Racing is big business, and it starts at a relatively young age.

1 One of the challenges for parents is knowing how much to encourage their kids to go faster. In some instances, parents can push their kids too hard and the kids will end up leaving the sport altogether.

2 Daniel Paluzzi is one of the fastest minibike racers in the country. Even kids this young are capable of doing 25-foot double jumps that are impressive to watch.

3 The major magazines only cover a handful of amateur events. In addition to the World Mini Grand Prix, the biggest event happens each year at Loretta Lynn's Dude Ranch in Hurricane Mills, Tennessee.

1 | Even amateur racers are extremely marketable. The Alessi brothers already have big deals with Honda, Bell Helmets, and Alloy MX gear.

2 The opening lap is very crucial in any race. Since most motos at the World Mini Grand Prix last 10 minutes, riders have to make passes early while all the riders are bunched together.

3 Kids start learning proper riding technique and body position as young as five. A good foundation allows them to climb on bigger bikes and adapt rather quickly once they are the right age.

1

1

As with any racing, a lot of the competitors show up on the starting line early to get a glimpse of course conditions. If the track is watered immediately before their race, they might want to change goggle setups and line choice around the track.

2

Lightning-fast reflexes are a must when the gate drops. When you are this far behind this early into a race, it's very hard to have any chance of exiting the first turn in the lead.

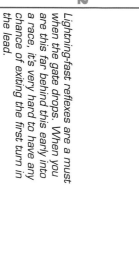

1 Suzuki signed Davi Millsaps after this season for more than a quarter million dollars. Not bad for a teenager making his pro racing debut.

2 Ruts can be helpful to larger bikes, but they pose a serious challenge for Pee Wee riders.

EL TRIAL DE ESPAÑA

ART ON TWO WHEELS

Name of Event:
El Trial de España
Location:
Temecula, California
Date:
April 25-27, 2003
Fan Attendance:
1,000

One of the oldest forms of competition is the sport known as trials. The goal is to tame a series of obstacles without putting a foot down, and do so faster than your competitors. This is extreme balancing at its finest, and it's nothing short of ballet on two wheels!

The bikes in this niche sport are unlike any you have probably seen before, and they are odd, to say the least. Built by European manufacturers like Gas Gas and Sherco, they feature ultra-narrow frames, small fuel tanks, high ground clearance, low seat height, and bicycle-like tires. The motors are low-revving and use torque, rather than speed, to climb obstacles that seem virtually impossible to overcome. Traction, too, is key, and the machines usually run less than three pounds of pressure to allow the soft tires to mold to any shape for ultimate adhesion.

El Trial de España takes place once a year, usually in the picturesque wine country of Temecula, California. This is considered one of the most popular trials events in America, and it attracts riders and spectators from all

Big gaps like this are incredible to watch in trials. Believe it or not, the rider starts this jump at a standstill, then gets his balance, puts the bike in a tall gear, revs the motor, dumps the clutch, and uses a lot of body language to clear the crevice. This is very technical and extremely dangerous, but the fans love it!

Results

Course Length: Multiple courses, each usually 100 yards long.

Terrain: Huge boulders, silt, and grass on a hillside and the surrounding valley basin.

Conditions: 60 degrees Fahrenheit.

Challenge: Searching for traction on the steep rock faces.

1. Geoff Aaron (4); 2. Ryon Bell (10); 3. Wilson Craig (16); 4. Chris Florin (18); 5. David Chaves (20).

over the country. They come not for the prize money, which is virtually nonexistent, but rather for the thrill of the sport.

There are fewer than 2000 trials riders in the United States, but you would never know it by talking to one of them. Their passion for the sport is unequalled, and they are purists to the bone.

Riders start with zero points at the beginning of each trials event. They run through a series of obstacle courses that are between 100 and 400 yards long and broken out into various degrees of difficulty. Novices and intermediate competitors are routed away from the dangerous or technical spots that are reserved for experts. Riders who make it through without dabbing (touching their feet or arms) are said to have "cleaned" the section and get zero points. Those who touch are awarded points, and the rider with the fewest points at the end of the day is the winner.

Most of the courses, such as El Trial de España, are run on courses created by Mother Nature. However, some are run on man-made obstacles constructed of metal drums, wood planks, pallets, used tires, and wooden spools. All of the action is done solo, like all the competition in the United States. But in Europe, the sport has become so popular that they have created a form of side-by-side drag-race-style competition that packs fans into 15,000-seat arenas. The obstacle courses are still very intense but are designed to thin the field through process of elimination. This adds to the drama and radically increases the speed and danger.

Whether competing indoors or out, trials is a sport about finesse, confidence, and determination. It mandates critical throttle and clutch control, a sixth sense for braking, and a keen eye for finding creative lines. Trials is also a sport of patience, experience, and technique. Unlike motocross, where it sometimes pays to ride on the ragged edge, such riding will only get you a lot of unwanted points and may injure a rider. The penalty for failing to climb a 20-foot rock face can be extremely painful. Perhaps that's why there seems to be more camaraderie here than in any other form of off-road competition. The riders are all in close quarters and walk the course together to seek out better ideas for achieving success. They look out for each other's safety, and many times will spot riders who are attempting something very risky.

1 Riding from rock to rock is very tricky because of the ground clearance of all motorcycles. In this section the rider, David Chaves, must use a "bunny hop" technique to make it through without dabbing his feet. This requires a lot of concentration and excellent hand-eye coordination.

2 This may look like a kamikaze move, but it's not. Riders use ultra-low air pressure to provide a lot of traction. When climbing something like this, it's important to keep the front end light, and then lean far forward once both wheels are on the rock face. This rapid body movement pushes the bike against the rock and helps out with traction.

3 Line choice and balance are important in this form of competition. The courses are extremely tight, and riders must know where the boundaries are at all times.

1

Each course is marked off using plastic tape and is usually 50-100 yards long.

This sequence shows what happens when you don't have a good drive. The rider, David Chaves, high-centers on the engine cases and then is forced to jump off his bike. Just before he let go, he gave the bike a forward shove which allowed a catcher to grab the bike so it didn't fall on top of him.

1 *Look closely at the front tire being squashed under pressure. Although these tires don't have big knobbies like those used in motocross, the soft-compound tire still provides incredible traction at these slow speeds.*

2 *Spectators are allowed within 10–20 feet of each course, and these huge boulders make for some interesting action.*

3 *Because of the slow speeds, photographers can search out all kinds of unique angles.*

Fans love trials because they can be just a few feet from the action. Trials riders rarely go faster than seven miles per hour, and the courses are usually in relatively small areas so fans can see all of the action.

Because trials take up little space and the bikes are quiet, many riders are able to build practice courses in their backyards. Riding on smooth ground and trying to balance at a dead stop can be a challenge for riders to master, but this type of control is necessary to be competitive even in the amateur classes.

"One of the neat things about trials is the cost," says Donnie Bales, an ESPN videographer. "If you do it right, a bike will last you a long time, and maintenance is fairly inexpensive. You don't go through as many tires, clutches, and top-ends like you do in other forms of motorcycling. You might bend your handlebar, tear a grip, or break a lever, but the investment is small when you look at something like GNCC racing where you need new tires every race, and will probably do $300–$500 damage to your bike in a race."

Riders don't need a specialized bike to compete in trials. Most events have classes for traditional off-road motorcycles straight from the showroom floor. Most of the adults who participate ride small bikes, such as a Honda XR100R or a Yamaha TTR-125 because they are easier to move in confined areas.

Age does not matter, and being physically fit is not as important in trials as in other forms of two-wheel competition. Riders only have two minutes to complete each section, and this makes practice and training less intense.

One of the most challenging maneuvers in trials is called a "splatter," in which a rider uses one obstacle as a liftoff point to jump over to another obstacle. This is similar to double jumping in motocross, but it is done at near walking speeds and requires a lot of aggressive body maneuvering.

"This is where experience comes into play," says Ken Faught, editor-in-chief of *Dirt Rider* magazine. "This is where the element of danger really hits home with the riders. This requires total concentration and commitment, and when executed perfectly, is the most rewarding thing for a rider."

"Strength is important in trials, but it's not as critical as in off-road or motocross," says multiple National Champion Geoff Aaron. "You really don't want to be overweight because it makes it harder to climb obstacles, but you don't have to have a lot of endurance. You have to be mentally tough, and you have to understand your limits. You have to trust yourself and know that you can place your bike where you want with pinpoint accuracy. This isn't a sport of feet or inches. It's a sport where millimeters count."

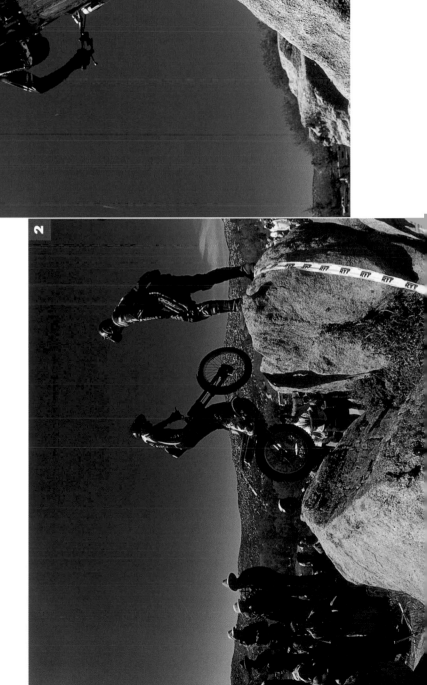

Even on flat areas of the course, the riders don't have time to rest. Although many can balance for a long time at a standstill, it takes a lot of energy and causes the motor to build up oil in the cylinder, which hinders performance.

2 A lot of the obstacles are narrow, in addition to being steep. This dramatically amplifies the challenge for guys like Wilson Craig who finished third overall in El Trial de España.

3 Course designers want to make the event difficult, but possible.

1

Trials is relatively safe because speeds rarely get over 7 miles per hour. This angle gives you an idea of how steep and slick some of the granite boulders were at the Southern California facility.

2

Where the front wheel goes, the rear wheel usually follows.

AMA NATIONAL CHAMPIONSHIP
MX SERIES

SIMPLY SPECTACULAR

Name of Event:
AMA 125/250cc National
Championship MX Series

Location:
San Bernardino, California

Date:
May 11, 2003

Fan Attendance:
20,000

Each spring, 20,000 fans flock to Glen Helen Raceway Park in Southern California for round one of the outdoor championship series. The high-speed, brutally tough 1.5-mile course is a perfect battleground for off-road riders. It's the best way to judge overall talent since it blends stadium-style jumps with uphills and roller-coaster descents. There are sandy sections, rocky sections, and sections with deep ruts. There are first-gear turns and third-gear turns, braking bumps and acceleration bumps, and screaming fans lining the entire course.

"The 'root of our sport is the outdoor series," says Davey Coombs of *Racer X* magazine. "This is the purest form of off-road competition, and we are fortunate that the fastest riders in the world now race in the United States."

The format of the 12-round series is simple. Riders compete in two classes divided by engine size. Younger riders typically ride in the 125cc class, while more experienced riders compete in the 250cc ranks. All riders who qualify for the 40-man main events compete in two races called motos that run for 30 minutes plus two laps.

"Basically each moto lasts about 40 minutes," says Donnie Bales, an ESPN videographer. "The top 20 riders from each moto earn points that count toward the championship. The rider with the most points at the end of the season is declared the champion."

Results Results Results

Course Length: 1 1/3 mile

Terrain: Combination of sand and loam. Big jumps, a 125-yard-long sand whoop section, and some of the steepest hills found anywhere in the world of motocross.

Conditions: 90 degrees Fahrenheit. The course was wet in the morning and then dried out during the afternoon.

Challenge: Avoiding fatigue in the hot California sun. The start is also critical since there are 40 riders in each of the 125 and 250cc classes.

125cc: 1. Mike Brown (Kaw); 2. Grant Langston (KTM); 3. Ryan Hughes (KTM); 4. Eric Sorby (Kaw); 5. Michael Brandes (Yam); 6. Bret Metcalfe (KTM); 7. Brock Sellards (Yam); 8. Stephane Roncada (Suz); 9. Chris Gosselaar (Hon); 10. Steve Boniface (KTM)

250cc: 1. Ricky Carmichael (Hon); 2. Chad Reed (Yam); 3. Tim Ferry (Yam); 4. Ezra Lusk (Kaw); 5. Kevin Windham (Hon); 6. Larry Ward (Hon); 7. Mike LaRocco (Hon); 8. Greg Albertyn (Suz); 9. John Dowd (KTM); 10. David Vuillemin (Yam).

In 2002, Team Honda's Ricky Carmichael became the first rider to sweep all 24 motos of the AMA 250cc National Championship MX Series. His brilliant performance defined dominance and intimidated the competition.

That winning streak continued into the 2003 event at Glen Helen. During the first moto it appeared that Carmichael was going to place second to Kevin Windham. Unfortunately for the Honda-backed four-stroke rider, Windham jumped off the track and fell over when his bike hit a pair of plastic barriers. Unhurt, Windham tried to kickstart his bike, but he couldn't get it going until 15 riders had passed him. Carmichael won that moto and the second as well. He is considered to be the fastest motocross rider in the world, but some say his only true competition races overseas.

By many accounts, Belgian Stefan Everts is the fastest rider on natural terrain courses. The son of Harry Everts, himself a World Champion, Stefan has amassed more Grand Prix titles than any rider in history. However, Everts doesn't like racing in the United States, and he's never had a chance to race against Carmichael on truly equal terms.

Some argue that the fastest rider may actually be James Stewart, riding in the 125cc class. Stewart, the defending National Champion, was absent from Glen Helen after he suffered a broken collarbone in a crash two weeks earlier during the 125cc East/West Shootout at the Supercross Series finale in Las Vegas.

The biggest question seems to be whether or not the 17-year-old could recover in time to be a title threat. Stewart had a plate installed in his collarbone to help it heal faster, but that only gave him 29 days to get up to speed. For Mike Brown, Ryan Hughes, and former World Champion Grant Langston, the absence of "Bubba" Stewart gives them an unexpected shot at the title.

1

1　At all national events, there are daytime qualifiers to get into the big show. For most of these riders, it will be their only chance to race in front of 20,000 people at an outdoor track, and the odds of making it as a factory rider are very slim.

"Stewart winning the title was almost a given," says Ken Faught, editor-in-chief of *Dirt Rider* magazine. "He's really in a league of his own. His innovative riding style is hard to beat, and he never seems to get tired. He's so surgically precise and consistent that he's got an incredible future ahead of him. With Jeremy McGrath and Travis Pastrana retiring, Stewart is probably the most marketable rider today."

Unfortunately, Stewart wasn't able to win the series, and the championship was decided under controversial circumstances. One of the rounds in Troy, Ohio, was postponed due to flooding and rescheduled as the last race of the season. Just five days before the new round 12 was set to happen, it was cancelled a second time. This was disastrous for Ryan Hughes, who had been engaged in a season-long title fight with KTM teammate Grant Langston. Hughes had a realistic shot to win the title at the season finale, but when the event was cancelled, Langston was awarded the coveted AMA No. 1 plate.

"I love all forms of motorcycle racing, but I think this series matters to me the most," says Eric Johnson of *Racer X*. "There's so much history here, and all of the tracks are so different. Glen Helen has its big hills, Red Bud and Troy have their jumps, and Southwick has its famous sand."

1 There are about two dozen really good factory rides available in the outdoor series, but there's a lot of support for the privateers. Kawasaki's Team Green program is one of the better known and takes an 18-wheeler and several technicians to key races.

2 Mechanics are also responsible for keeping their riders calm, cool, and collected throughout the day. A solid working relationship is a must between a riders and their mechanics.

3 The fastest riders get the first pick on the starting line. Here, multiple champion Ricky Carmichael has chosen the inside line because it's usually the shortest route and the safest, if there is such a word in racing.

4 Mechanics like Brent Myron work 18 hours on race day to keep the bikes in top mechanical shape. Throughout the day, it's common to go through six to eight tires, a clutch, and three air filters.

1

But the National Championship Series has changed dramatically. The top riders who once traveled to the races in regular vans have long since disappeared. Self-financed privateers who log 55,000 miles annually in box vans park only a few feet from million-dollar semi trucks. These factory-backed rigs are nothing short of race shops on wheels. Inside, there is typically a million dollars worth of spare parts to rebuild the $100,000 race machines. These exotic parts are expensive because of their costly development time and small production runs.

"These trucks are absolutely amazing," says Mike Gosselaar of Team Honda. "I have more than enough parts to keep Ricky Carmichael's bike going at all times. We also restock the truck after every single race, so we're quite prepared."

"Our semis are pretty much self-contained," says five-time World Champion Roger DeCoster, who now manages Team Suzuki. "We have one truck for our 125 team and another for our 250 riders. Each truck has its own bathroom, generator, and water tank, along with several pressure washers. We have areas to rebuild motors, modify suspensions, and hold team meetings. Up in the lounge area, we have a television and VCR so we can watch tapes from practice. The riders use this valuable tool to evaluate lines and look for ways to reduce lap times."

Team Sobe Suzuki usually has 27 team personnel at the races to help the seven factory riders. "I remember when riders only had one mechanic and a shared team manager," says three-time World Champion Greg Albertyn. "Now each team has its own suspension technician, motor development guy, truck driver, and in most cases, some type of trainer or sports doctor. There's definitely a lot of support, and it just goes to show how much the title is worth to a manufacturer."

Inside reports indicate that Carmichael earned almost $6 million in 2002 for his supercross title and his perfect National Championship season. "I'm fortunate that I really don't have to pay attention to the money anymore," says Carmichael. "I did at first, but now I've surrounded myself with a lot of good people who look out for me. I've seen a lot of riders get distracted by chasing after the buck, and I'm fortunate that I can just focus on racing and winning."

1 In the search for traction, riders lean way back on their fenders at Glen Helen. This track has one of the longest starts, over 200 yards, and the dirt is very loose and bogs down the engine.

2 At Glen Helen, riders like Chad Reed reached 65 miles per hour—almost double the speeds found in stadium racing.

1 Flying debris makes goggle prep a must. Most riders use three to six tear-offs on their goggle lenses to keep them clean. Tear-offs are thin pieces of plastic that can be pulled off during a race to expose a clean under-layer.

2 Greg Albertyn came out of retirement at Glen Helen and placed eighth overall. The former three-time World Champion and 1999 AMA 250cc National Champion could be competitive today, but he's got a new career: The South African is raking in millions of dollars as a home builder.

1   Mount St. Helens is one of the biggest descents on the 12-race National tour. It's full of incredibly steep braking bumps, which cause fatigue.

2   Motocross racing is generally closer than supercross, because the obstacles are spaced much farther apart.

3   The first turn has been dubbed Talladega by race fans because its banking represents something that would normally be found at a NASCAR event. This allows for incredibly high speeds, and lot of commitment on the part of the rider.

1 The promoters of the Glen Helen National import dozens of truckloads of sand to make the track more challenging. This section is over 100 yards long, and the top riders like Ricky Carmichael had no problem with its ever-changing surface.

Marketing is now a huge part of this sport, and for good reason. With motorcycle sales tripling in the last eight years, many consider motocross to be the most visible sport in which people can compete on a realistic budget.

France has a lot of incredibly fast riders like Sebastien Tortelli, David Vuillemin, and Stephane Roncada shown here.

1

1

Fan interaction is a big part of racing. All of the top riders sign autographs for at least one hour a day, and the teams hand out posters and custom stickers.

2

Ezra Lusk has had a few tough years since his glory days as a member of Team Honda. After the 2003 season, Kawasaki gave him his walking papers and for 2004 he'll ride for a satellite Yamaha team called Mach 1 Motorsports. It may be a cut in pay and prestige, but satellite teams can often extend the career of a solid top-20 rider.

ADVENTURE RIDES

THE GREAT SHORE LUNCH QUEST

Name of Event:
Canadian Shore Lunch Quest

Location:
Elliot Lake, Ontario

Date:
July 16, 2003

Fan Attendance:
15 crew members, 25 support staff, and 2 tourists

T hat ain't gonna fly," eight-time National Champion Dick Burleson said, tugging the straps holding a 2004 450EXC on to the left float of a 1955 DeHavilland Beaver. "We need to build a hard mount."

He headed to his truck, dug through the drawers full of tools and parts, and came up with an aluminum bar. Riders Mark Frederick and Jeff San George jumped into the fray, helping Dick heat and bend the bar to fit. It was then mounted from the handlebar to the plane with scrounged bolts and a washer found in the plane owner's shed.

"Now that," Dick said, eyeing his work with satisfaction, "isn't going anywhere."

The kind of ingenuity shown by Burleson is part and parcel of a day in the dirt on a motorcycle adventure ride. On these trips, off-road riders can combine their love of being on two wheels with a desire to see new places. The concept is nothing new, as riders have been traveling on bikes since the dawn of the motorcycle. The allure of such a ride, however, has become more and more popular in the past 10 years.

Sales of dual-sport motorcycles—street-legal motorcycles that can handle off-road terrain—have grown steadily and manufacturers such as KTM and BMW offer a variety of machines built specifically for adventure riding. Dual-sport bikes allow riders to use roads legally and greatly increase the options for riders.

1 *This camp on Beef Lake is deep in the wilderness near Elliot Lake in Northern Ontario and was supposedly impossible to get to by trail. We made it, but a fly-in would be a lot simpler way to fish this gorgeous place. Lee Klancher*

2 *Guide Darryl Beamish cooks up freshly caught lake trout for a shore lunch. Lee Klancher*

3 *The Elliot Lake area is great for canoeing and is probably one of the only places where canoeists and dirt bikes share trails. Lee Klancher*

4 *Bugs were "not bad," meaning they were plentiful and hungry. When the bugs are "bad" in Ontario, you have to hide under netting (seriously). Lee Klancher*

Results

Course Length: 25 miles

Terrain: 10 miles of car-width two-track running along a hilly, rocky power line; 15 miles of tight single track winding through cedar and poplar forest, with creek crossings and trails running over rock faces.

Conditions: Nearly perfect; 70 degrees Fahrenheit and sunny. Two-track was just a bit dusty, and the woods trail was damp black loam with good traction. Some deep mud and ruts in lower, swampy sections of trail. Rocky sections were dry and clean.

Challenge: The navigation was the most difficult part of this ride, as the trail was not marked. Toughest section to ride was a narrow, muddy, rutted climb winding through tight poplar trees; deep slippery ruts also tricky to navigate. Fields of Pomeranian-sized rocks required good bike handling skills, as well.

Four 2- to 5-pound lakers (lake trout) netted and pan-fried by our fishing guide!

Bikes are loaded with gear, and riders head off deep into wilderness areas that offer plenty of trails and scenery. Popular destinations include Baja California, where riders can travel the rugged Baja 1000 race course and hundreds of miles of nearly unmarked trails, Colorado's network of fire roads cutting across the state's mountains, and Virginia's Hatfield-McCoy trail system.

The experience doesn't require an exotic destination, however. Any national forest with off-road motorcycle access is a prime spot for an adventure ride.

Navigation becomes a big part of the experience, and knowing how to read a map or a global positioning system (GPS) is key. Dual-sport events are becoming increasingly popular, and the more organized of these offer downloadable GPS tracks.

Another big challenge is finding fuel. Adventure bikes are typically equipped with oversized fuel tanks, which give a 100- to 150-mile range. In the wilds of Baja, where gas stations sporadically open and close, riders who have not planned carefully can find themselves stranded in the desert.

Commercial adventure tours often offer adventure rides. Tour operators around the world take riders into the wilds of Australia; Baja California; Moab, Utah, South America; and Africa. In fact, pretty much any exotic destination now has a tour operator who can take you into the back country on two wheels.

These operators provide bikes, guides, and support trucks. All a rider has to do is show up and write a check and they're off on the adventure of a lifetime.

My favorite adventure trips are those done on my own, with a loosely planned route. The challenges are greater, as you are typically running without the safety net of a support truck and have to plan your trip, but the discoveries on the trail always seem to be worth the extra risk and effort.

The Canada adventure in July 2003 came about as a result of my friend Mark Frederick and I's quest for a great shore lunch. We had cooked up the idea the previous fall, dreaming of riding to a

1

Thousands of miles of backcountry trail cut through the bush country north of Elliot Lake. This giant pile of sawdust is all that remains of a logging operation, and is now a popular stop on a bush trip to Hell's Gate Rapids. Lee Klancher

2

The last half-mile of our journey took place in Darryl Beamish's fishing boat. Captain Dick keeps watch for the island where lunch and the crew are waiting. Lee Klancher

3

The trail ride back was a bit more relaxed, as we knew the route and that we could make the trip without a problem. Lee Klancher

remote lake, catching a mess of fish, and frying them up on the shore. We tried that on Minnesota's North Shore, and didn't catch a fish.

I tried again in May 2003 on an ATV trip in Canada, and was skunked again on a remote trout lake. Our guide told us we arrived too late to catch fish, and we found ourselves eating sandwiches rather than fresh fish.

For the third attempt, we brought along a camera crew to film an episode of *Dirt Rider Adventures*. The hosts of the show, editor Ken Faught and actor and off-road rider Molly Culver, were flown in to join us. *Dirt Rider* correspondent and riding hero Dick Burleson brought brand-new KTMs along, as well. With this big crew on hand, I enlisted several local guides and a float plane to help us in our quest for a meal of fresh fish.

One of the guides took us back to Beef Lake, a remote trout fishing lake in the wilderness near Elliot Lake, Ontario. The area is a prime destination for ATV riders, with 200 miles of marked trails surrounding the town of approximately 12,000 souls. That extensive trail system accesses area gas

1 | *Never follow too closely when your buddy is crossing a stream. Jeff gets an unwanted bath from Mark's CRF.* Lee Klancher

stations, hotels, restaurants, and even the mining museum. With only a handful of maintained roads and 4,000 lakes in the Elliot Lake region, this was prime country for off-road exploration.

We had heard conflicting reports about the trail we would be riding to Beef Lake. Some of the locals said it was an easy ride, while others swore we could not get there on motorcycles. Everyone agreed that the trout fishing was good. An impassable trail with good fishing at the end? Adventures don't get much better than that.

The float plane, loaded with a brand-new KTM 450EXC and show hosts Ken Faught and Molly Culver, was our backup plan. They would get to the lake, even if the tough trail hung us up.

We also had guide Darryl Beamish flown in ahead of time to scout the lake and nail some lakers. Dave Hendrickson, the owner of Laurentian Mountain Outfitters and the Beaver, assured us that Darryl was the best guide in the area.

The fish didn't have a chance this time.

We left the plane and mounted KTM, and Dick, Mark, Jeff, our guide, and I hit the trail to Beef Lake. The first 10 miles of trail were part of the myriad of trails around Elliot Lake, Ontario.

The highline trail we started on was open and fast, with a few turns and rocks and lots of interesting little playgrounds on the side. We found a few rocky steps to climb, and a sandpit with a fun little jump—nothing radical, but good fun.

We came to a bridge, and stopped to wait for our guide. Dick immediately began tinkering with his KTM, a 250EXC four-stroker with a Thumper Racing 300cc kit.

"You have a baggie or something?" he said. He had lost a bit of fluid to the hydraulic clutch, and filled it up with a splash of gasoline from the tank. Dick is as relentless wrenching as he is riding, which is saying a lot.

We came to the turn-off into the bush, off the open trail on the highline. The guide showed us the trail that led to Beef Lake and pulled out of the way. "Have fun," he said.

We did just that. The trail was narrow and nearly grown over, with a smattering of stumps and rocks hiding in the weeds. Deep ATV ruts crossed soft ground that would be impassable muck in the spring, but had receded to hub-deep goo in the mid-summer heat.

A couple of stream crossings featured fist and softball-sized rocks under 12 inches of copper-clear Canadian water. When we stopped, the mosquitoes were fierce. I wondered how Californians Ken and Molly would deal with the bugs. I had warned Ken about the bugs, and even bought him a bug hat (a mesh bag that fits over your head, keeping the bugs away).

After about eight miles of the trail, we started working our way down to the lake. We wrapped around the lake, and came out at a landing where, according to the plan, a boat would be waiting for us. We found nothing but an old rowboat overturned in the brush with two battered oars lying next to it.

"Is this our boat?" Jeff asked.

Considering the steady wind blowing out in the main part of the lake, we sincerely hoped not.

Dick, never one to sit still, pointed to a narrow rock peninsula just across from us.

1

"If I ride to that," he said, "Would you take a picture?" Before I could answer, he and the 300 disappeared into the under-growth. We could hear the sound of the four-stroke thumping, and brush snapping as he rammed his way through the thicket.

Jeff couldn't stand it, and fired up the 250EXC and headed after him.

Fifteen minutes later, DB emerged and rode out to the point. He pumped his fist and pointed, indicating that he could see the guys at the camp. Jeff emerged shortly after, about 200 yards behind Dick. The thick brush proved more than he wanted to tackle, so he decided to cross the lake. The shore was steep and log-filled, and Jeff was quickly headed into deep water. Once the vent tubes went under, the bike ran poorly and didn't want to start. Visions of sinking the only KTM 250EXC available to the North American press ran through my mind.

Thankfully, DB stepped in and gave Jeff a bit of help, and the bike came out of the drink. Shortly after, our guide, Darryl Beamish, showed up in a small boat, and took us across to meet Ken and Molly and the rest of the crew. Ken was glowing on the dock, full of stories about an incredible flight in the float plane. The KTM made the flight without a scratch, as Dick's fabrication held it on securely.

Molly, the host of *Dirt Rider Adventures*, had flown in as well, and was having a great time checking out the shore lunch preparations. She also told us that Ken had spent a good part of the last day eating bananas, which she thought was hilarious. Eating bananas makes you tastier to mosquitoes (or so the legend goes).

Ken, swatting at a buzzing horde, looked over when we started laughing. "What??" he said, slapping at his neck.

We were running late, and didn't have time to fish on Beef Lake. Our guide had come through, however, and had caught seven lake trout and put them immediately into an ice-filled duffle bag. He filleted off thick, pink-tinged slabs and fried them in two cast-iron pans over an open fire. They were flaky, hot, and delicious.

After the meal, we rode back to the trucks, stopping to play on the rocks on the way. On the last leg, in the warm glow of the early evening sunlight, I watched as Dick, Jeff, and Mark bounced over the Canadian rocks and turns ahead of me. The ride transformed the world into nothing more than line choices, shift points, wheelies through puddles, and staying loose in the rock fields.

That night, over dinner, we ate big meals and downed a few cold ones in the lovely log dining room of the Laurentian Lodge. Stories were told and retold, and we basked in the glow that comes after an adventure to remember.

1 Beef Lake, at last! The island with our crew and shore lunch is just across Beef Lake. Jeff San George discovered his 2004 250EXC was not up to crossing the lake. Lee Klancher

2 Water crossings are part of the trail system in the Elliot Lake area. Jeff San George is seen here crossing one small river successfully. Lee Klancher

Adventures can be found in the unlikeliest places. This one began with Mark and me loading up the bikes on a quest for a shore lunch in northern Minnesota. Maybe if we had caught a few walleyes and fried them up, that's where it would have ended.

But life rarely works out the way you plan it, and we didn't catch that fish. I came to Elliot Lake last May on an ATV trip, still looking for a shore lunch. I found a place that has become one of my favorites and good people that I now consider friends, but missed out on the shore lunch again.

The third time's the charm, it seems, when it comes to shore lunches. Thanks to Darryl, on the shores of Beef Lake we sampled the finest fresh trout I have ever tasted.

Adventures, great and small, are one of the great pleasures of life. Whether the quest is finding fish in Canada, chasing kangaroos in the outback, or looking for the perfect dive bar in Park Falls, Wisconsin, they always yield good times, great people, and stories worth telling.

When you do them on two wheels, life doesn't get much better.

1

Eight-time National Enduro Champion Dick Burleson took to the trail en route to Beef Lake. Dick is one of the legends of the sport. Now in his 50s, he still rides like a demon. Lee Klancher

HOW TO TALK CANADIAN, EH?

Note that most of these references are to beer or fishing. I'd say that's just a sign that Canadians have their priorities straight.

A boot: about

Eh?: end sentences with this expression ("How a boot a quick Mickey, eh?")

Forty: 40-ounce bottle of booze

Loonie: Canadian dollar coin

Mickey: small bottle of booze

Mouthpiece: someone who talks too much (most Americans)

Peelers: strippers

Pickerel: walleye

Pogey: welfare or employment insurance

Poutine: fries, gravy, and lots of cheese

Puck Bunny: hockey player's girlfriend

Speckles: brook trout

Toonie: two-dollar coin

Tuque: winter cap

Twenty-sixer: 26-ounce bottle of booze

Two-Four: case of beer

1 The cable television show Dirt Rider Adventures (Outdoor Life Network) was on hand for the Canadian adventure. Host Molly Culver gets a bit of a splash from riders Mark Frederick and Jeff San George as part of a segment of the show. Lee Klancher

1

The rocks provided some challenging climbs, but nothing that DB and the rest of the crew weren't up for. Our television crew, which chased the riders on ATVs, had a bit more of a challenge navigating the obstacles. Lee Klancher

2 Ken Faught and Dick Burleson stop on top of Beaver Mountain, overlooking the Elliot Lake area. This overlook is accessible from the Elliot Lake trail system, which runs through the town and features about 300 miles of ATV-friendly trails. Lee Klancher

1

A good adventure ride features plenty of nearly impassable obstacles. In this case, Burleson had to search out this wicked log crossing about 20 yards off the trail. It took DB 10 attempts to figure out a way to cross the log cleanly, and both the bike and rider were steaming afterwards. Lee Klancher

2

Some of the trail on the route to Beef Lake was well packed and ran on top of the hills in the area. This kind of riding was simple enough and gave us a chance to take in the area's scenery. Lee Klancher

GREAT AMERICAN
CHAMPIONSHIP HILLCLIMB

BORDERS ON INSANITY

Name of Event:
Great American
Championship Hillclimb

Location:
Billings, Montana

Date:
July 26-27, 2003

Fan Attendance:
20,000

The most dramatic form of motorcycle racing takes place annually in the small town of Billings, Montana. Each July, a couple hundred riders bring their home-built machines to the base of a 420-foot hill in the quest to make it over the top.

The land is owned by the Billings Motorcycle Club, which has promoted the event since 1918. As many as 20,000 spectators watch the drama as the two-day event unfolds, and it's always spectacular.

"It's not a matter of if you are going to crash, it's a matter of where," says Karel Kramer of *Dirt Rider* magazine. "Only a handful of riders make it over the top each year, and it all depends on weather conditions and how the hill has eroded during the last year."

"No one is allowed to ride on the hill except during this event," says BMC's Darrell Devitt. "This way the hill doesn't get worn out, and everyone has an equal shot at getting over the top. It doesn't matter if you are from Florida or right here in Billings, no one gets any practice time, period."

1 Jeremy McGrath borrowed a 218-horsepower Harley-Davidson and a modified Honda CR500 from Team Peterson. He placed fifth and ninth in the normal classes, and second overall in the Montana State Shootout. Ken Faught

Results Results

Course Length: 420 feet

Terrain: Steep uphill comprised of bentonite

Conditions: Wet in the mornings and dry in the afternoons

Challenge: Finding the right time and getting a lucky start number. The course changes dramatically throughout the day, and the course "comes in" and "goes away" in as little as 15 to 20 minutes.

State Championship: 1. Travis Whitlock (13.564 seconds); 2. Jeremy McGrath (13.769); 3. Larry Coleman (14.113); 4. Harold Waddell (14.172); 5. Shannon Chamberlain (14.744); 6. Brandon Whitlock(14.762); 7. Jon Smith (15.107); 8. Mel Kimball (15.771); 9. Pat Liscum (15.952); 10. Pete Krunich (18.109).

0-600: 1. Travis Whitlock (14.806 seconds); 2. Mel Kimball (15.416); 3. Harold Waddell (15.436); 4. Pete Krunich (15.550); 5. Jeremy McGrath (16.121); 6. Jon Smith (16.487); 7 Shannon Chamberlain (16.529); 8. Eric Cherry (16.668); 9. Jay Coffey (16.692); 10. Dusty Beer (16.748).

0-700: 1. Jeff Thomas (271 feet); 2. Ed Taylor (258); 3. Travis Whitlock (257); 4. Dusty Beer (253); 5. Brandon Whitlock (252); 6. Nolan Martin (250); 7. Jon Smith(248); 8. Shannon Chamberlain (247); 9. Jeremy McGrath (247); 10. Jason Smith (246).

Open 1: 1. Travis Whitlock (12.418 seconds); 2. Larry Coleman (12.639); 3. Harold Waddell (13.210); 4. Robbie Peterson (14.491); 5. Dave Johnston (14.808); 6. Pat Liscum (15.043); 7 Shannon Chamberlain (15.151); 8. Kurt Koester (15.271); 9. John Cullinan (15.729); 10. Ed Taylor (15.769).

701-Up: 1. Brian Osborn (13.476 seconds); 2. Travis Whitlock (15.436); 3. Jeff Thomas (15.796); 4. Brandon Whitlock (16.390); 5. Chad Lorenz (16.909); 6. Scott Ehlers (17.032);7. Ed Taylor (18.528); 8. Devin Aymond (18.882); 9. Scott Olson (19.662); 10. Nolan Martin (22.304).

Seniors: 11. Dave Johnson (18.754 seconds); 2. LeRoy Ebling (378 feet); 3. Ken Long (353); 4. Dean Cromwell (352) 5. Doug Sherburn (349); 6. Karel Kramer (348); 7. Lefty Frueh (188);8. Dave Chizzone (180).

Participants have the opportunity to ride in a number of classes, and each entrant gets two runs per class. Most of the racing is run through a notch at the top of the hill, but others go up an even steeper area.

"The zero to 600cc class draws the most entries because of the rules," says Kerry Peterson, a five-time world champion. "To make hillclimbing more affordable, the organizers created this class where nearly stock Kawasaki KX500s and Honda CR500s rule the earth. Riders are allowed to extend their wheelbase to 66 inches, which is about a foot longer than stock. The added length makes the bikes less likely to flip over backwards. Combined with a wider tire with every other row of knobbies

2 Robie (shown) and his brother, Bret, are from the legendary Peterson family. Their father, Kerry, owns several world records aboard custom-built Harley-Davidsons, like this 2500cc monster: Karel Kramer

removed, riders are able to increase traction. In the past, riders used steel paddles or as many as 150 carriage bolts protruding out from the inside of the tire to increase traction, but these were eliminated in 2002 for safety reasons.

"There are not too many standards in the unlimited class," adds Kramer. "About the only thing these bikes have in common are two wheels and a handlebar. I've seen everything from three-cylinder snowmobile engines to Harley-Davidson V-twins shoved into home-built frames. Robie Peterson even has a Honda 1000 with two CR500 motocross engines run in tandem, but doesn't run it any more."

Street bike engines are common in the modified classes because of their compact engine design and the fact that they have room for a countershaft sprocket, unlike car engines. Travis Whitlock runs a 110-horsepower Yamaha FJ1200 motor, and that's the type of muscle needed to be competitive at the top level. Robie Peterson, son of Kerry Peterson, rides a 1340cc nitro-burning V-twin Harley that cranks out 200 horsepower. And if that's still not enough, Robie has a 2500cc Harley.

"It's really interesting walking through the pits," says seven-time AMA Supercross Champion Jeremy McGrath. "There are all sorts of weird things out there. It's amazing what these guys will build in their quest to climb that hill. I would never be caught dead on some of the bikes, but there are also some really good bikes out there. All of the stuff built by Kerry Peterson seems to be like works bikes, and Travis Whitlock has some really good equipment as well."

"We don't have a lot of rules," adds Devitt. "Riders need to have a helmet, at least one brake, a dead man kill switch, and no more than two tires—that's the key. We don't allow any bike sharing, and you can subtract from the tire, but no material can be added."

Participants begin their day with a riders meeting at the bottom of the hill. Start positions are drawn from a hat, which is the only way to make it fair, since conditions on the hill can change dramatically within minutes. Members from the BMC begin laying out the course on Saturday morning.

"A few years ago, *Dirt Rider* invited Larry Roeseler and Ty Davis to join us at this event," says Kramer. "Ty saw a guy carrying a bunch of small flags and asked what they were for. I told Ty they were marking the course, and he turned to me and said, 'What? We don't get the whole hill?' It was pretty funny, because he and Larry are some of the most talented off-road riders in the sport's history, and even they had a hard time figuring out the hill. Neither got over the top their first year, and the only time LR made it over the top the following year, he had to get off and push. It's a lot more difficult than it looks. Photos really don't do this place justice."

1

Over 20,000 spectators turn out over the two days of racing. They flock around the "Key Hole" which is a burnout area for riders to clean out their engines before making the adrenaline-filled run. Ken Faught

"This year we thought it would be interesting to invite Jeremy McGrath," says Ken Faught, editor-in-chief of *Dirt Rider* magazine. "Jeremy saw me do it on television and wanted to know what it was like. I made some calls, and ended up getting him dialed in with the Peterson family. Like most families in this sport, they are very friendly and willing to do whatever they can to promote the sport. And having McGrath show up at a race like this is just unbelievable. The buzz in the pits has been intense ever since he came through the front gate."

"This really makes me nervous," says McGrath. "I watched videos for two hours at Ken Faught's house, and saw a bunch of ugly crashes. I know it can be done; I just have to figure out the technique. I'm really not afraid of the climb, but I'm horrified of the fall."

"It can be 10 seconds of terror," says Robie Peterson. "For starters, the clean-out area has this huge sign that says, 'Welcome to the Bentonite Nightmare.' That's enough to put the scare in anyone. Then, on the return run, you get to look at the guy in front of you, and that usually means watching him cartwheel. Then you roll your bike up to the base of the hill and wait for the okay to go. The hill is always

3

2

changing, so it's really important to watch new lines develop and old ones go away. Then you cross your fingers, pin the bike in second, and hope everything goes your way."

"There's usually no shifting," adds Kramer. "You really don't have a lot of time to build speed. The hill is so steep that it robs a lot of power, and you rarely see anyone go over 20 miles per hour except in the shootout. That's because they remove all the flags and give riders a straight shot at the notch, and this is when guys can get going 40 miles per hour. It's pretty spectacular."

Another usual sight at Billings is the catchers on top of the hill. These are brave men and women who protect the riders at every cost.

"These guys are nuts," says Faught. "They use big 5-pound hooks attached to ropes to catch out-of-control bikes. Even though the catchers wear hard hats, chest protectors, and boots, they can get hurt pretty bad. If it wasn't for them, I don't think most of the riders would try the wall, because it's almost suicidal. Nothing good is going to happen when a 300-pound bike lands on top of you after falling 20 feet."

2 Harold Waddell finished fourth in the 0-600cc class, but failed to make the top 10 in any class aboard this streetbike-powered Suzuki. Ken Faught

3 Riders start at the base of the hill without any run. Building speed and keeping your bike pointed straight is incredibly important to have any chance of making it over the top. Ken Faught

Of nearly 1,000 individual attempts, there are usually 15 to 25 riders who make it over the top.

"It's an incredible feeling making it over the top, especially your first time," says local racer and past champion Dusty Beer. "You can hear the crowd screaming, and you know that you have done something special."

Riders who don't make it over the top are awarded a score measured in feet. Those who make it over the top are timed electronically with photo sensors.

"One year, the hill got so gnarly at the top that they had a guy literally jump over the sensor," says Kramer. "They had to relocate the finish line sensor about 30 feet down the backside of the hill to make sure that didn't happen again."

The winner of the Great American Championship Hillclimb gets a portion of the $35,000 prize money and the satisfaction of knowing that he's done something truly special.

1

This is one dangerous situation. The safety crew hates it when riders let go of their bikes in mid air. Fortunately, the bikes are equipped with a device that automatically kills the engine once the rider lets go of the handlebar. Ken Faught

2

Maintaining control the entire time is difficult. Just moments before this photo was taken, Travis Whitlock hit a small ledge buried in that crevice the locals call "the chute." It was one of the few runs where Whitlock didn't make it over the top. Ken Faught

3 Look at that beefy rear tire very closely. Apply horsepower to that baby and you can see how this rider ended up in this ugly predicament. Ken Faught

4 The safety crew at Billings does a great job of keeping riders out of harm's way. Ken Faught

5 To make the hill more challenging, course designers cut ledges into the face of the hill. Ken Faught

1

Former GNCC Champ Shane Watts tried his hand at hillclimbing in 2003 and didn't fare so well. He broke the swingarm of his borrowed KTM as his suspension bottomed out at the steepest section of the hill. Ken Faught

2

You can't afford to lose your balance for too long. Just after this photo was taken, the rider lost control and tumbled down the hill. Ken Faught

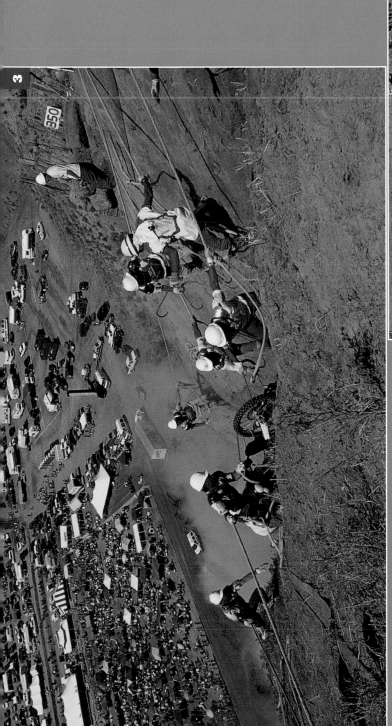

1

1

Jon Smith wasn't the only rider to get out of control at the top of the hill. Notice the guy with the video camera running for cover next to the hay bales. The finish line is 20 feet down the backside of the hill, and riders throw roost up to 50 feet once they get on the throttle. That's also the main reason the safety crew wears those hard hats. Ken Faught

2

Colorado's Travis Whitlock and his home-made Yamaha FJ1100-powered machine are an incredible combination. He's the greatest rider of modern times, and proved that by beating supercross phenom Jeremy McGrath. Ken Faught

24 HOURS OF GLEN HELEN

ENDURANCE DEFINED

Name of Event:
24 Hours of Glen Helen

Location:
Sab Bernardino, California

Date:
September 6-7, 2003

Fan Attendance:
20,000

Preparation is required for every race. For motocross and supercross, the bikes are built for peak performance at the expense of durability. After all, motors are torn apart after every two to three hours of use and critical parts are replaced. But what happens when the race lasts for 24 hours?

"Everything changes," says Dave Chase of Pro Circuit. "You have to build a bike that won't fall apart, literally. Everything has to be safety-wired together or Loc-Tited down. You need to check every bolt to make sure it's snug, and then check it again. You can't leave anything to chance. You want to factor in performance, but it's way different than motocross. You don't want arm-jerking power; instead, you want smooth power that won't wear you out."

"We spend a lot of time building our factory bikes," says Team Honda's Johnny Campbell. "We try to find the weak points, and then fix them. We do a lot of testing before ever racing a bike like the

1 The 24 Hours of Glen Helen is one of the most demanding races on man and machine. Many of the teams, including this one sponsored by Dirt Rider Magazine, fail to finish because of motor or electrical problems.

2 Pit lane is open to spectators and safety is a big concern. The 5-mile-per-hour speed limit is strictly enforced, and the competitors look forward to the relaxed pace down the 250-yard section of the track.

3 This shot from a hill near the course shows the pits at midnight and the town of San Bernardino, California, in the background.

4 Joe McKimmy's team was running third overall until the motor expired.

Results

Course Length: 8 miles

Terrain: The once-a-year course design combines the normal motocross track with the Grand Prix course and several hills in the surrounding areas. It's full of silt, hard-pack dirt, a dry creek section, and one mile of asphalt near the Blockbuster Pavilion, an open-air concert arena.

Conditions: Dry and dusty

Challenge: Keeping a bike running for 24 hours, and avoiding problems with makeshift light systems at night.

1. Ty Davis/Ryan Dudek/Terry Fowler/Nathan Woods; 2. Johnny Campbell/Steve Hengeveld/Andy Grider/Spud Walters; 3. Ty Renshaw/Jason Abbott/Sean O'Connor/Tim Sharp.

XR650R, but it doesn't stop there. After every race we tear the bikes down to the frame to see firsthand how everything withstood the abuse. We look for irregular wear, cracks, chips, or anything unusual. This dedication helps us build future race bikes, and helps Honda build better production machines."

The annual event at Glen Helen Raceway in San Bernardino, California, is unusual in the world of two-wheel competition, blending the nighttime thrill of the infamous 24 Hours of Le Mans with the nasty terrain common in the Baja 1000. It's a real rock-around-the-clock where riders team up in groups of six for amateur classes or groups of four for the professional class.

The race starts and finishes in daylight, but it's the nighttime that has the greatest appeal. "It's an unbelievable feeling to ride in total darkness," says motojournalist Donnie Bales. "You have to put a lot of trust in your equipment. If your lights fail, you can really get hurt. That's why a lot of guys run two separate light systems—one that runs off the power generated by the motorcycle, and a totally separate system that runs off batteries. This way if one fails, you have a redundant system. I've actually been at races where guys have crashed and couldn't find their bikes for 30 minutes because of the darkness. People forget that when the engine dies, the lights go out, because most dirt bikes don't have batteries; however, that too seems to be changing. With electric-starting off-road bikes becoming more common, very compact batteries are making their way onto the scene."

"Some people claim they can actually go faster at night," says eight-time ISDE gold medalist Dick Burleson. "They feel that way because they can't see all the scary stuff, and sometimes that's true. It's real easy to get tunnel vision when riding at night, and that lets you concentrate more on going fast. It's really a cool experience."

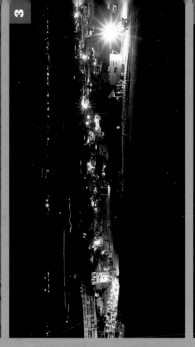

5 M. P. H. ONLY

1

The course is very dry because of a water shortage.

2

Ty Davis and his Yamaha-backed team win the overall.

3

Off-road legend Ty Davis is almost as fast at night as he is during the day. Many consider Davis one of the most versatile off-road riders of all-time.

"There are a lot of things you have to look out for," says Baja's winningest rider, Larry Roeseler. "You have to make sure you keep your lights pointed in the right direction. It can be really hard to see when you jump, and timing is difficult if you choose to wheelie over obstacles. You really have to watch out when riding at night because shadows change everything. Some things look bigger while others look smaller. You really have to have a lot of practice in order to go fast, but it's amazing just how powerful lights have become."

Pit strategy also plays an important part in the overall picture of endurance racing.

"You want to have everything planned so you can spend as little time in the pits as possible," says Campbell. "You don't want to make mistakes because they can easily cost you a win. You want to have all your spares ready, know who's in charge of refueling the bike, when riders are switching off, and always have someone inspecting the bike for broken parts before they have a problem."

1

2

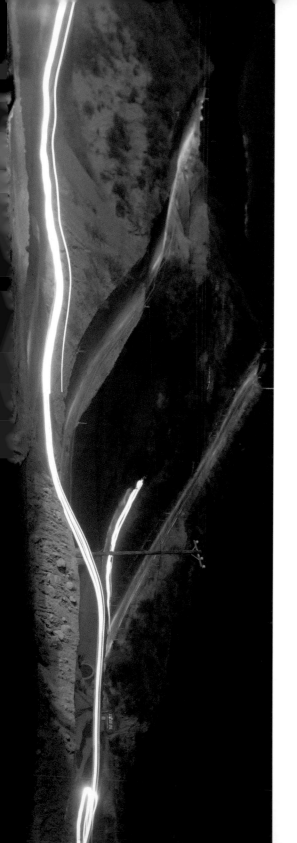

1 *Competitors do a complete lap around the motocross track, and the entire track is the same at night as it is in the daytime.*

2 *This is a family event where everyone has a job. The Dougherty boys ride the bike while dad handles the pits and coordinates all the logistics.*

3 *Most teams begin with an off-road bike such as this KTM EX/C that comes stock with headlights, unlike most motocross bikes which can be difficult to modify for night riding.*

"There are a lot of things that you can do to make a bike better suited for this type of competition," adds Bales. "Most riders use larger gas tanks and run heavy-duty tubes or Bib Mouses [solid foam inserts that replace inner tubes] to prevent flat tires. Ideally, you want to start the race with a new chain, sprockets, and brake pads, because all of these parts will sustain heavy wear during a 24-hour event."

Depending on conditions, most teams will replace tires and air filters several times during the event. Pit stops also give the riders time to make adjustments to suspension and carburetor settings, get a fresh pair of goggles, and fill up their drink system. During a race like this, it's not uncommon for a rider to drink two to three quarts of water an hour and expel the water in the form of sweat.

"Staying hydrated is very critical," says Ty Davis, a multiple Baja winner. "You can't get enough water in your system. It's also very important to eat in between your shifts on the bike, so you have plenty of energy to charge during the entire race.

"There's a whole different mindset when entering a race this long," says Davis. "You have to think about making the bike last and riding at a pace you can sustain. A lot of riders have a tendency to sprint at the beginning, but that will only wear you out and increase the chances of crashing and damaging your bike. You want to establish a pace that you can

1

For some teams, the list of problems seems to be endless and confusing. There are only a handful of races worldwide where motorcycles race around the clock.

2

When a racer enters the pits, there's a job for the entire crew, including the other riders. At the very minimum, the bike needs fuel, the rider needs water, and his goggles must be cleaned or replaced.

3

Most teams experience several problems through the race. Some problems can be easily fixed while others can be catastrophic.

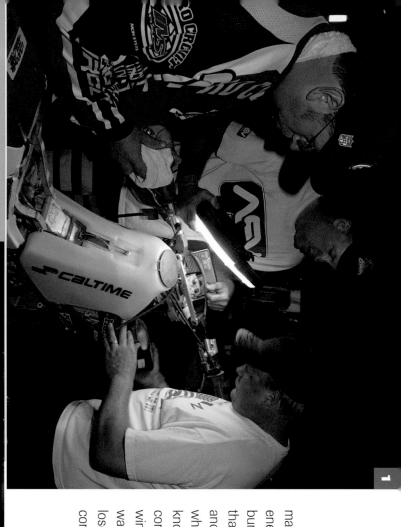

maintain, and then try to have a little extra energy in reserve, just in case you have to bump up the pace at the end. We make sure that our pit crew keeps tabs on our progress and that of our competitors, so we know where we stand at all times. That way, we know whether or not we can afford to ride conservatively or must ride aggressively to win. If you have a big lead, the last thing you want to do is crash trying to go fast and then lose the race. That's where strategy really comes into play."

DAY 8

125

The course varies in speed, terrain, and conditions, yet spectators usually limit their movement to the pit area and motocross track in order to get a glimpse of the riders.

DAY 9

INTERNATIONAL SIX DAYS ENDURO

THE WORLD'S TOUGHEST OFF-ROAD RACE, PERIOD.

Name of Event:
International Six Days Enduro

Location:
Fortaleza, Brazil

Date:
November 3-8, 2003

Fan Attendance:
4,000 (450 riders)

The International Six Days Enduro (ISDE) has long been considered the Olympics of off-road motorcycle racing. The ISDE is the dirt bike equivalent of the decathlon. Just as the winner of the decathlon is considered the world's greatest all-around athlete, the winner of the ISDE, or Six Days, is considered the world's best all-around dirt bike racer. As its name implies, Six Days subjects the best riders in the world to six consecutive days of a staggering variety of challenges. The ISDE is held in a different country every year, and its racers ride an average of 150 miles a day at a brisk pace in order to arrive at the checkpoints on time—too late or too early, and they're penalized by the minute.

But that's not the tough part.

Most of the top guns can maintain the required trail pace with little problem, so to separate the contenders from the pretenders, ISDE organizers set up a number of special tests. These are generally serpentine courses two to four miles long over natural terrain that are sort of like old-school motocross tracks. Riders tackle these one at a time and are timed for only one lap—fastest time wins. There's no practice allowed on any part of the course, though riders may walk any portion and most competitors walk each test in order to get that critical mental picture of how they'll attack it when it's time to turn a wheel on it.

But wait, there's more!

Results

Course Length: 817 miles (1314 km) over six days

Terrain: Sand, dunes, rocky, dry fields, and rocky single-track trail up and down the jungle mountains.

Conditions: Hot and humid.

Challenge: Surviving the week without crashing out, hitting a car, or seizing the engine in the sugary sand while avoiding dehydration.

Overall Individual: 1. Stefan Everts (Belgium); 2. Stefan Merriman (Australia); 3. Juha Salminen (Finland).

Trophy Team Order: 1. Finland; 2. Italy; 3. France; 4. Spain; 5. Australia; 6. Germany; 7. United States; 8. Czech Republic; 9. Poland; 10 Mexico; 11. Belgium.

First-place rider: Stefan Everts

Junior Trophy Team: 9th

Top American was Kurt Caselli: 17th.

Ty Davis: 19th

Mike Lafferty: 38th

Mike Kiedrowski: 41st

Jason Raines: 48th

David Pearson: 51st

Rodney Smith: 141st

Robbie Jenks: 83rd (highest placing club rider for United States)

GNCC Club Team: 2nd overall Club

Results

Almost 80 years old, Six Days has its roots in a time when motorcycles were not reliable—keeping one running for nearly an entire week was a feat in itself. (In fact, when the British came up with the idea for this game, they dubbed it the International Six Days Trial, and it certainly was a trial to keep a bike going for six days.) Not only must the rider go as fast as possible in the tests and keep up a brisk pace on the rest of the course, they must also be able to perform the necessary mechanical tasks required to ensure that the bike lasts. No one is permitted to help the rider work on the bike, other than topping off fluids (fuel and coolant, for example) or airing up tires. It's up to the rider to change air filters, worn tires, or any other parts, and do so without any help (other than shouted advice). If something major breaks, it's up to the rider to disassemble, repair, and reassemble the motorcycle—and it must be done within the 10-minute work periods at the beginning and end of each day or at any checkpoints if the rider gets there ahead of time. Failure to do so means clocking in late and losing points.

At the end of the week, everyone's scores are compiled, and since it's basically a race against the clock instead of each other, the lower the score, the better. While Six Days is a race comprised of many individuals, the individual results aren't as important as the team scores. Every racer represents their

1 *The ISDE determines the world enduro team championships yearly, and since it's held in a different country every year, it also takes on a different character every year.* Mark Kariya

1

It's all about the results, though the top three individuals are also honored. From left are Finland's Juha Salminen (third place), Belgium's Stefan Everts (first place), and Australia's Stephan Merriman (runner-up). Mark Kariya

2

Since ISDE courses encompass much of the countryside, it's common for transport sections to be crowded with local spectators, as they are here watching American Club team rider Lars Valin. Mark Kariya

1

country and is placed in one of the four team categories. Most prestigious of these are the six-rider World Trophy teams, the best of a country's best. Next in line are the four-member Junior World Trophy teams; these are comprised of riders younger than 24. Those who aren't members of the more elite categories generally are part of a three-rider Club team. There are also three-member teams representing manufacturers; they, however, don't have to be from the same country. (Also, a rider can be on a manufacturer team plus another team, but that's the only combination permitted—no Trophy team riders on a Club team or Juniors on the Trophy squad.)

Though the United States produces some of the finest motorcycle racers in the world, Americans have not enjoyed much success at Six Days, with a best World Trophy team finish of second place (Czechoslovakia in 1982). How is this possible? Primarily because this European game is so much different from the way enduros are run on U.S. soil.

You see, American enduros (as well as hare scrambles, hare and hound desert races, and GNCCs) place a premium on endurance. Yes, it takes a bit of endurance to ride for six days in a row, but the way the ISDE has evolved, today especially, the determining factor is sheer speed in the tests.

"We don't know how to get on the edge for the tests," six-time AMA National enduro champion Randy Hawkins admits bluntly. "All [the top Europeans] are superfast for one lap, and that's it. All [of us Americans], from [racing] GNCCs and enduros, everybody gets to a pace, and they ride the pace that you can ride for three hours or a hundred miles (which is how long the average National-caliber American off-road race is).

"The ability's there. It's just that we don't have a mindset of turning it up to 110 percent for [five] minutes (which is how long it takes to complete the average special test). I just think that's something we don't do enough of, and it shows."

But occasionally, Americans see a ray of hope, most often on those rare occasions when Six Days ventures away from its European base. The 78th ISDE was one of those occasions, as it visited Brazil, the first time the race was held in South America; the U.S. hosted it twice (1973 and 1994), as did Australia (1992 and 1998).

The Brazilian ISDE of 2003 was based from a beach resort near Fortaleza, which is a popular tourist destination in the northern part of the country. Hot, humid and, above all, sandy, it promised to be very different from the usual Six Days—European versions are often cold, wet, and muddy.

The conditions helped level the playing field, many Americans felt, but so did the fact that the Europeans faced unfamiliar logistical challenges that Americans deal with every year. Except for the home team and a few neighboring countries, all competitors put their bikes, tools, spares, and pit supplies into shipping containers several months ahead of time. They don't have the luxury of working out of familiar

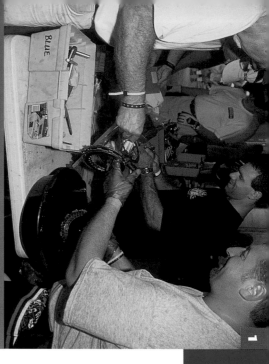

score of the event. (Davis, commendably, was just 40 seconds behind him for 10th in class and 19th overall.) Caselli has a bright future should he wish to pursue Six Days and says that would suit him just fine: "For sure I want to do some more. I don't know if it's something I'm going to do every single year. We'll see; I want to go to different places, I want to see the world, so I think it's a good opportunity to get around and race and ride in different places." (The U.S. Junior World Trophy team finished ninth out of 15.)

Of course, if the United States is to be considered a real threat in the Olympics of off-road motorcycle racing, it will need at least six racers who can run the pace, be mechanically adept, and function in a team setting. Americans generally seem to rise to such challenges, and it'd be oh so fitting to match the superpower status America enjoys in the official Olympic Games.

1
Even the volunteer support personnel need to prepare. In this case, Lindsay Pirie (left) and Jim Corsello prepare a spare clutch. Only riders can work on bikes during the race. Mark Kariya

2
As U.S. Club team rider Mike Sigety is doing here, every competitor also needs to figure his schedule to ensure arriving at checkpoints on time. Mark Kariya

3
Special tests—electronically timed to the hundredth of a second—usually begin and end in the same area for logistical considerations. U.S. Club team rider Luke McNeil takes off here. Mark Kariya

4
The ISDE is won or lost in the tests so it's crucial to go as fast as possible. U.S. Junior World Trophy team rider Wally Palmer uncorks. Mark Kariya

1

GNCC champion Jason Raines turned in the fifth best performance among the Americans, earning a gold medal in only his second Six Days. Mark Kariya

2

Trails are where riders spend the majority of the six days; they help define the country from the rider's view. Eric Bee (No. 325) zips down a Brazilian mountain trail. Mark Kariya

3 Desert racer Kurt Caselli felt at home in Brazil's sandy special tests, helping propel him to eighth in class and 17th overall, best of the Americans. Mark Kariya

1 Brazil provided many different views not normally seen at Six Days, which is usually held in Europe. U.S. World Trophy team member Mike Kiedrowski passes the water park. Mark Kariya

2 Maintenance must be performed by the rider; in this case Ty Davis. Others, however, can aid the rider, as Kenny Parry is doing. Mark Kariya

3 There's no time for lunch so racers must refuel their bodies with snacks throughout the day. Providing these snacks is the job of the support personnel. Mark Kariya

LAKE ELSINORE GRAND PRIX

RACING FOR ANYONE AND EVERYONE

Name of Event:
Lake Elsinore Grand Prix
Location:
Lake Elsinore, California
Date:
November 8-9, 2003
Fan Attendance:
5,000

Two days a year, the sleepy town of Lake Elsinore, California, is transformed into a 5-mile off-road course. Thirty years ago the town 90 miles south of Los Angeles was immortalized in the hit film *On Any Sunday*, as Malcolm Smith and Steve McQueen raced through town at freeway speeds. Today, over 1,500 entrants participate in the event, and it's now one of the most popular off-road races in the country.

As many as 125 riders turn out for each 45-minute grand prix, which starts on Main Street. The course winds through town in front of mom-and-pop-owned businesses and small single-family homes half a century old. It snakes around the surrounding hill-sides on two-track roads, before dropping onto another paved section. There are two high-speed fire roads, a street crossing, a man-made tabletop jump, an ultra-fast sprint across a bridge over Interstate 15, and the famed water-hole jump.

"Speeds out here can reach 100 miles per hour for some of the bigger bikes," says Team Green's Destry Abbott. "This race is really unique because it's 25 percent street, and most of the course is lined with spectators. A lot of people turn out for Lake Elsinore because it's so unique and because it has such historical importance.

"Elsinore is a classic," says veteran pro motocrosser Mike Healey. "It's not uncommon to see people ride five or six classes and spend a thousand dollars in entry fees and hotel rooms. This is really good for the local economy, and it's totally free for spectators."

"The locals really seem to love this place," says Jerry Robinson, an amateur racer. "A lot of businesses say that this is their best week of the year. Some will rent out their parking lots for race teams to use, kids will pull out their garden hose and wash bikes for five bucks, and all the restaurants are filled with racers in full riding gear. Motorcycling really does take over this town in early November."

"The high speeds really make bike prep important," says Dave Chase of Pro Circuit Racing. "It's real critical to change gearing so you can do 80-100 miles per hour. You also want to run a steering stabilizer to reduce headshake and allow you to charge at things more aggressively. Flats are also a problem at Elsinore because there are a lot of rocks littering the course, so it's a good idea to run heavy-duty inner tubes, and sometimes even that is not enough!"

"Four-strokes really seem to be the hot tip here," says Steve Hatch of Team Suzuki. "The smooth power works

1

GFI
L. ELSINORE
MOTORCYCLE
GRAND PRIX
EVENT
STREET
CLOSED AHEAD

1
This event is one of the few races in the United States where city streets are closed for racing.

2
Upwards of 150 riders begin each 45-minute race.

Course Length: 5 miles

Terrain: This event is run down Main Street in Lake Elsinore and has several other asphalt sections that connect the dirt portions. There is a huge tabletop jump that is a spectator favorite and a double jump over the water hole.

Conditions: Extremely high speed (some riders hit 100 miles per hour), and the track was wet most of the weekend.

Challenge: The course is filled with a lot of partially buried rocks that puncture tubes.

100 Mile Final: 1. Lance Smail; 2. Scott Sheak; 3. Bobby Bonds; 4. Scott Myers; 5. Joey Lanza; 6. Michael Lapaglia; 7. Elmer Symons; 8. Brian Brown; 9. Mikey Childress; 10. Robert Fouls; 11. Troy Lee; 12. Rob King; 13. Ben Hale; 14. Tyler Duncan; 15. Tyler Keefe; 16. Dusty Nabor; 17. Kelly Yancy; 18. Dan Hallada; 19. Kyle Beshaw; 20. Dean Price.

Results

1

The riders start in waves of 30-75 riders at a time, and it's interesting to watch them navigate the asphalt on knobby tires.

2

There are several sections of the course where the riders transition from dirt to asphalt. If you look closely, the riders are actually landing on a normal city street that is covered by a lot of dirt that has been tracked onto its surface.

really well at high speeds on the slippery turns. The weather here is really unpredictable, and the course can get really greasy when it rains."

The biggest race of the weekend is the Harvey Mushman 100, named after the alias used by actor Steve McQueen in the 1970s. It's a 100-mile race that lasts three hours. Most racers use oversized gas tanks, and even then, they still have to pit a few times for fuel. While in the pits, which run next to the curb on Main Street, riders also get fresh goggles, a drink of water, and occasionally make setup adjustments. Hydration is very important, and for that reason most riders carry a drink system on their back that can hold several quarts.

"The event is not that physically demanding," says former Grand National Cross Country Champion Shane Watts. "The course really doesn't get that rough. There are a lot of sections where you can rest, and I think that's what attracts a lot of riders. Desert races can wear you out quickly, and so do enduros and cross-country races, but this GP isn't that brutal on man or machine."

"The distance isn't that bad," says Scott Sheak, a former pro motocrosser turned off-road rider. "Anyone who races desert is used to racing for several hours, but guys who normally race motocross usually struggle with the time. It's important to keep a positive attitude and stay

1

1

This huge tabletop jump is the biggest leap on the course and draws the most spectators.

2

During the big 100-mile race, riders make several pit stops to get fuel, clean goggles, and have a drink of water.

1

focused. You can't let your mind wander, otherwise you might do something stupid out there. This course is fast, and it's easy to get in trouble in a hurry."

"I'm always excited for this race," says promoter Goat Breker, a one-time factory Kawasaki motocrosser. "It's one of the most historic motorcycle races in the country, and everyone always has a good time. It's not tied into any one series, so riders from motocross, off-road, desert, road racing, etc., all get to come out and do battle against one another with no real pressure."

"The whole atmosphere at Elsinore is incredible," says KTM's Kelly Yancey, one of the few women racers. "A lot of people stumble across this race by accident, and they are impressed at what they see. I always get a bunch of people coming up and asking me why I do it. It's hard to convey the real fun, but I think they see it on my face."

"My family and I make it a weekend every year," says Tiffany Harper, a spectator. "My husband and I bring the kids out, and it's always enjoyable. We get to meet a lot of friendly people, and we're not even involved in the sport. We don't ride motorcycles, but we have a lot of fun watching."

"Our goal is to make sure it remains a family sport," adds Breker. "We want to use this event to showcase our sport and prove that motorcycle riders are good people. We always seem to get a lot of positive feedback after the event, and that's really why we do it. We really don't do this for the money, because it's very expensive to promote."

"I've talked to people that have driven from New England to race here," says John Hunter, a spectator. "With the popularity of this race, I'm surprised there aren't more of them like it across the country."

1 Off-road legend Scot Harden used this event to test out his big-bore 950 for the famous Paris-to-Dakar rally. In the 6000-mile rally, Harden was in the top 10 before breaking his leg during the final third of the three-week race.

2 Even on the dirt, speeds can reach 75 miles per hour.

1

Riders are assigned starting positions about 20 minutes before their race, and the open pits allow spectators to interact with the competitors.

2

After several hours of racing, most riders get blistered hands, making it painful to hold onto the handlebar.

3

This is one of the two residential sections where the racetrack has been fenced off. In the past, spectators would try to cross the street on foot, which is incredibly dangerous...and dumb.

4

The course is 15-20 feet wide, and there are classes for almost everything, including ATVs, vintage bikes, and dual-sport machines.

1 Believe it or not, this is a 450-pound BMW streetbike, but the course is so fun that people can't resist racing whatever they've got.

2 Scott Sheak won this event in the past, but he finished second to Lance Smail in 2003.

1 The asphalt sections can be extremely tricky. If you get off line in areas that have dirt on the surface, it is easy to lose control.

2 The Lake Elsinore Grand Prix gets a lot of television coverage. In 2003, Ken Faught covered the event for Outdoor Life Network and Spike TV from the racer's perspective.

3 Some pit stops are faster than others for a variety of reasons. Here, the team removes the tank to work on a serious motor problem.

INDEX